# CQB

by
Mark V. Lonsdale

**Additional Books by
Mark Lonsdale**

*Raids
SRT Diver
Sniper Counter Sniper
Advanced Weapons Training*

# A Guide to Unarmed Combat and Close Quarter Shooting
by
Mark V. Lonsdale

## DISCLAIMER

The author, STTU and those that contributed to this book take no responsibility for the use or misuse of the material herein.

C.Q.B. was written as a guide for qualified and experienced law enforcement or military personnel, with no intention of contradicting their current agencies' policies.

Unarmed combat and special weapons training are potentially dangerous activities that could lead to serious injury or death, if not properly organised and supervised. The training methods indicated in this book should only be under-taken by selected and trained personnel, under the strict supervision of qualified instructors and team leaders. Each and every individual involved in special operations training should act as a Safety Officer, and be constantly alert to any potential safety violations.

No moral or legal conclusions should be drawn from any of the following material. We have tried to present the mechanics of unarmed combat and special weapons training, leaving the legal and policy decisions to the individual agencies concerned.

All training should be under the control of qualified instructors and all operations under the control of qualified commanders.


CQB

First Printing January 1991
Second Printing January 1992
Copyright © 1991 by Mark V. Lonsdale
Los Angeles, California 90049

All rights reserved. No part of this book may be used, reproduced, stored or transmitted in any manner whatsoever, without written permission of the publisher.

ISBN 0-939235-03-X

Library of Congress Catalog Card Number 90-92330

PRINTED IN THE UNITED STATES OF AMERICA

# DEDICATION

To the men and women of the Special Operations community—who must periodically enter the arena . . .

"The credit belongs to the man who is actually in the
arena, whose face is marred by dust and sweat and blood . . .
who knows the great enthusiasm, the great devotions;
who spends himself at a worthy cause;
who at best knows in the end the triumph of high achievement;
and . . . if he fails, at least fails daring greatly so that his place
shall never be with those cold, timid souls who know
neither victory nor defeat."

John F. Kennedy

*"It is fatal to enter war
without the will to
win it."*

Douglas MacArthur

## AUTHOR'S NOTE

Through-out my career I have shared many interests with my peers and associates, in both military and law enforcement circles. One common bond that I have found with all, is a certain job satisfaction drawn from working in close proximity to danger. Whether in advanced tactical training, or on operations, there is always the (often unspoken) thrill that comes with putting one's training and abilities to the test.

To quote some unknown operator, "The months of boredom, interrupted by seconds of sheer terror."

As one matures, the search for excitement is still there, but one finds safer and sometimes more satisfying past-times. Mine has become teaching. The opportunity to pass on much of the information and experience that has been bestowed upon me over the last 20 years.

Nothing would please me more, than to spend the next 20 years working with every special operations team in the free world from the newest recruit to the most experienced operator. Whether through classroom lecture, demonstration or hands-on training; to share my personal experience, years of training and research, and concepts for modern special operations and training.

Unfortunately, time, money and commitments will make this impossible. I hope, through these books, I will be able to stimulate thought, present alternatives and encourage training, with teams that also lack the time and resources for formal training.

There is no substitute for realistic training, but I also understand that few teams get the budget or opportunity to train to optimum levels.

This book represents only one view, one method, one training philosophy. Although many will consider this material invaluable, the reader must continue to be open to other ideas and methods. The criminal and terrorist world is a constantly changing arena—one that requires tactical flexibility in all operations, and therefore training. Seek out the best training programs, keep what is suitable for your arena, and store the balance for future reference.

Training material, to be of value, must be first understood, applied in training and then used on operations. It is not sufficient to just know the theories. Only through realistic application can new material become an operational asset.

In conclusion. To all my faithful friends and readers; soldiers, sailors, marines, police, sheriffs and special agents; the ones that share my enthusiasm for special weapons and tactics, and encourage me to write more—I sincerely thank you.

## ABOUT THE AUTHOR

All S.T.T.U. operations come under the direct control and supervision of Mark Lonsdale, an internationally recognized advisor on police and military special operations.

Mark has over twenty years experience in martial arts, combat shooting, tactical training and special operations. He received his black belt in judo at age sixteen and went on to compete in three world championships, before joining the military. By the early eighties, Mark was ranked in the US Top Ten combat shooters; was twice winner of the French International and a member of the US team to the European Championships.

As Director of S.T.T.U., Lonsdale continues his work in special operations training, law enforcement diving and international diplomatic security. His close association with US and overseas agencies, combined with T&E work for the US arms industry, helps to keep the S.T.T.U. training material current and interesting.

**Current Status:**
Director—S.T.T.U. Training & Studies Group
FBI and NRA certified Police Firearms Instructor
Spec. Ops. Coordinator—NASAR Diving & Water Rescue Committee
SCUBA Diving Instructor/Instructor Trainer—UCLA/NAUI
Civilian Diver—LA Sheriff's/SEB Marine Company
Advisor to several law enforcement and military agencies
Member NASAR, ALEA, IACP, IADRS, NAUI and the Republican Party

**Alan Brosnan**

12 years military experience
9 years attached to N.Z. SAS
Assault group commander
Military demolitions/explosive entry instructor
Counter Terrorist/close quarter battle instructor

**Jack Sims**

7th Dan Black Belt in Karate
Head of the Chidokan Karate Association (23 years)
CQB Instructor for the Elite N.Z. SAS
Police unarmed combat instructor
Certified firearms instructor

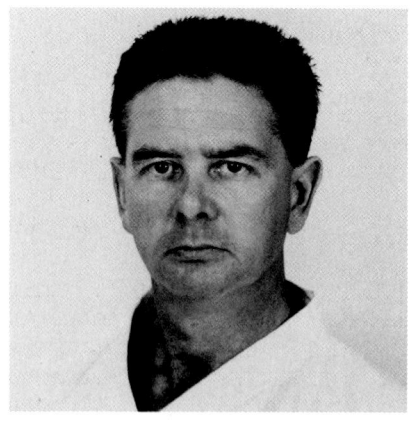

**Bryan Fitzpatrick**

5th Dan Black Belt in Karate
Chidokan Karate instructor, 1970-1978
Assistant instructor in CQB for N.Z. SAS
N.Z. open karate champion, 1968-1978
Police and military CQB instructor

# HISTORY OF STTU-CQB

STTU's CQB program was developed at the request of several police and military agencies, and represents a life-time of experience in martial arts, combat shooting and special operations.

STTU's program is the product of three men's work over the last two decades. Each coming from different fighting disciplines and backgrounds, but eventually meeting and combining their knowledge into one truly effective close quarter fighting form.

Mark Lonsdale began Judo at age 11, attained his Black Belt at sixteen, his 2nd Dan at seventeen, and went on to compete in three World Championships before his twenty-first birthday. Almost two years of his judo career was spent training in France, at the National Sports Institute and RCF, where he succeeded in winning three national team titles.

In his mid-teens, Lonsdale also became involved in hunting and high-powered rifle competition. This was sacrificed for more intensive judo training and international travel, but served him well for his military service. During Basic and Advanced Infantry Training and his Infantry Officers' Course, Lonsdale excelled in weapons training and held the position of top rifle shot. Continued cross training in karate, aikido and boxing maintained his interest in the martial arts.

Upon leaving the Army, Lonsdale attended the Commercial Diving Center in Long Beach and went on to become a deep sea diver in the North Sea oil fields. It was during this period that Mark was introduced to combat pistol shooting, and by 1982 had made the US Top Ten—going on to be twice winner of the coveted French International, and member of the US Team to the European Championships. It was also in 1982 that Lonsdale turned his attentions back to special weapons training, taking up his current position as Director of S.T.T.U.'s Training & Studies Group.

In the last several years, Lonsdale has trained and studied with police and military Special Response Teams throughout the western world. His books have become standard texts for many involved in hostage rescue, criminal intervention and counter terrorism.

On the other side of the world, a young karate player by the name of Jack Sims, returns from a successful training session in Japan (1967) to found the New Zealand Chidokan Karate Association. This was after seven years of judo, jiu-jitsu and karate training, and teaching martial arts at Auckland University.

In 1977 Jack was awarded the rank of GODAN (5th Dan), the highest Master rank within Chidokan Dan grade system. But it was back in 1968 that Jack was contracted to develop and run a special 'close quarter battle' program for the New Zealand Army's elite Special Air Service (SAS). This proved to be the first in a series of courses run for the SAS and their CQB instructors. This program has been constantly researched and upgraded throughout the years, and is still in operation today, some twenty-two years later.

Being only passing acquaintances from their early martial arts careers, it was not until 1984 that Mark and Jack came together in New Zealand. Mark eager to study Jack's karate methods and CQB program, and Jack keen to learn Mark's advanced close quarter shooting techniques and hostage rescue drills. 1984 and '87 took Lonsdale to the South Pacific to work with Jack and his staff; 1988 brought Jack Sims and his senior instructor, Bryan Fitzpatrick, to the United States for special weapons and tactics training. Both groups benefited from the exchange.

It was during Lonsdale's second visit to New Zealand, to attend one of Jack's SAS-CQB programs, that he met the third contributor to the current STTU program. Alan Brosnan was a CQB Instructor and Assault Group Commander for the SAS; a nine year veteran of the squadron with twelve years of international military experience. Alan's work with the NZSAS, British SAS and other elite counter terrorist teams, gave him a unique perspective as to exactly what was needed by teams in both a conventional and CT role.

Upon leaving the military in 1989, Alan took up the position of Chief Instructor for S.T.T.U., and began applying his experience to teaching US law enforcement and military teams. Alan's experience as a CQB Instructor, and background in boxing and karate, has made his assistance invaluable in preparing and teaching the STTU-CQB and explosive entry programs.

# INTRODUCTION

CQB is the fourth in a series of books based on the training methods of the SPECIALIZED TACTICAL TRAINING UNIT and serves to complement the material presented in previous texts, ADVANCED WEAPONS TRAINING for Hostage Rescue Teams and RAIDS.

CQB (Close Quarter Battle) is a guide to advanced armed and unarmed combat techniques developed specifically for police and military hostage rescue teams. This book, as with any book, is not designed to replace hands-on training but will be of value to all police, military and government personnel involved in special operations (Spec-Ops).

STTU's unarmed combat techniques are a combination of several fighting styles with a foundation in Shotokan Karate, Judo and Aikido. Only the most effective techniques have been adopted and then carefully modified to suit the counter terrorist/hostage rescue role. All techniques are intended for close quarter engagements where more conventional fighting and shooting styles may not be suitable. In addition, CQB covers such topics as:

> close quarter shooting with handgun, shotgun and submachine gun; advanced individual unarmed combat; essential team drills for room combat; weapons retention during hostage rescue drills; attack and defense with edged weapons; hostage and prisoner considerations; structuring a training program and instructor development.

CQB should be essential reading for not only operational personnel and assault team members but also administrators, unit commanders, procurement officers and tactical instructors. Apart from SWAT/HRT teams, this text will benefit undercover agents, drug enforcement officers, high risk warrant service teams, military police and regular patrol officers. The techniques illustrated are easy to grasp, quick to learn and effective to employ.

This book is not intended to replace a comprehensive training program, sweat and hard work, but simply to stand as a reference and source for offensive and defensive close quarter techniques uniquely suited to tactical operations.

## ACKNOWLEDGEMENTS

Many agencies and individuals have contributed material for use in the S.T.T.U. programs. Too numerous to name here, but they know who they are and have my deepest appreciation. Those that deserve special mention for their contribution to CQB are:

> Jack Sims, Chidokan Karate Association
> Alan Brosnan, Chief Instructor—STTU
> Bryan Fitzpatrick, Chidokan Karate Association
> Ben Griffiths, Chidokan Judo/Aikido Instructor
> Neil Parker, Chidokan Karate Association
> Dave Watson, Weapons & Explosives Instructor
> Karen Lewis, STTU Marketing
> Bill Hahn for his excellent cartoons
> John Satterwhite, Heckler & Koch

## PHOTOGRAPHIC CREDITS

The photographic material in this book is the work of Mark V. Lonsdale. Those photos depicting the author were done with the assistance of: Alan Brosnan, Karen Lewis and Dave Watson.

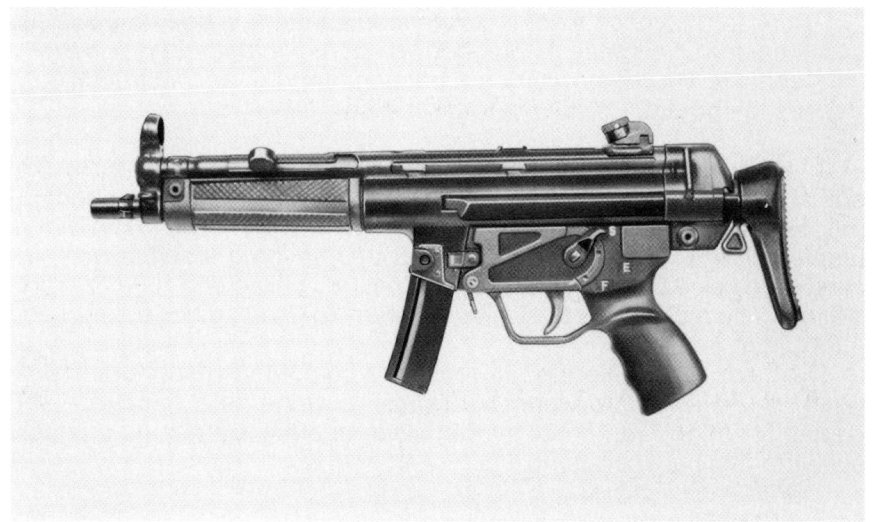

# CONTENTS

## I PREPARATION

1 **OVERVIEW** . . . . . . . . . . . . . . . . . . . . . . . 1
   Role of CQB in SWAT/HRT Operations
   Shooter Back-up
2 **TRAINING CONSIDERATIONS** . . . . . . . . . . . 7
   The Team
   The Instructor
   Training Locations
   Training Equipment
   Program Design
3 **PRINCIPLES OF UNARMED COMBAT** . . . . . . . . . 17
4 **MENTAL CONDITIONING FOR SELF DEFENSE** . . . . . . 21
5 **HUMAN ANATOMY** . . . . . . . . . . . . . . . . . 27
   Vital & Vulnerable Areas
   Natural Weapons of the Human Body

## II UNARMED COMBAT

6 **FIGHTING FUNDAMENTALS** . . . . . . . . . . . . 37
   Stances
   Balance
   Movement
7 **STRIKES & BLOCKS** . . . . . . . . . . . . . . . . 41
   Sparring
8 **KICKS** . . . . . . . . . . . . . . . . . . . . . . . 55
9 **JOINT LOCKS AND BREAKS** . . . . . . . . . . . . 61
   Joint Locks
   Breaks
   Control Techniques
10 **THROWS** . . . . . . . . . . . . . . . . . . . . . 67
   Break-falls
11 **CHOKES & STRANGLES** . . . . . . . . . . . . . . 73
   Warning
12 **DEFENSE AGAINST IMPACT WEAPONS** . . . . . . . 79
   Short Weapons
   Long Weapons

**13 EDGED WEAPONS** . . . . . . . . . . . . . . . . . . . . . . . **83**
    *Knife Attacks*
    *Knife Selection*
    *Knife Defense*
    *Warning*

**14 GUN DEFENSES** . . . . . . . . . . . . . . . . . . . . . . . **97**
    *Handgun Defenses*
    *Long Guns*

## III NON-LETHAL OPTIONS

**15 ASSAULT CONSIDERATIONS** . . . . . . . . . . . . . . **109**
    *Explosive Entry*
    *Stun Munitions*
    *The Assault*
    *Safety*

**16 NON-LETHAL OPTIONS** . . . . . . . . . . . . . . . . . **115**
    *Introduction*
    *Baton*
    *Impact Projectiles*
    *Gas*

## IV CLOSE QUARTER SHOOTING

**17 INTRODUCTION TO COMBAT SHOOTING** . . . . . . . . . **125**
    *Historical Perspective*
    *State of the Nation*

**18 THE WEAPONS** . . . . . . . . . . . . . . . . . . . . . . **129**
    *Handguns*
    *Submachine Guns*
    *Shotguns*
    *Ammunition*

**19 SAFETY AND FUNDAMENTALS** . . . . . . . . . . . . . . **143**
    *Safety*
    *Training Progression*
    *Fundamentals of Combat Marksmanship*

**20 CLOSE QUARTER SHOOTING** . . . . . . . . . . . . . . **153**
    *Principles of Close Quarter Shooting*
    *Changing Focus*
    *Beyond Accepted Principles*
    *Speed*
    *Mental Preparation*

**21 ROOM COMBAT** . . . . . . . . . . . . . . . . . . . . . . . . . **169**
    Basic Tactics
    Areas of Responsibility
    Target Engagement
    Shot Placement
    Verbal Communications
    Failure Drills

**22 WEAPONS RETENTION** . . . . . . . . . . . . . . . . . . . **181**
    Safety
    Training

**23 POST SHOOTING MANAGEMENT** . . . . . . . . . . . . . . **195**
    Domination
    Hostage Considerations
    Prisoner Handling
    Medical Considerations
    Command Debrief
    Post Shooting Investigation
    Critique

**24 CONCLUSION** . . . . . . . . . . . . . . . . . . . . . . . . . . **205**

**Appendix A** . . . . . . . . . . . . . . . . . . . . . . . . . . . . . **207**
    ADDITIONAL READING

**Appendix B** . . . . . . . . . . . . . . . . . . . . . . . . . . . . . **209**
    GLOSSARY OF TERMS

**Appendix C** . . . . . . . . . . . . . . . . . . . . . . . . . . . . . **211**
    SUPPLIERS / ASSOCIATIONS

**Appendix D** . . . . . . . . . . . . . . . . . . . . . . . . . . . . . **215**
    MODIFIED BRIEFING PROCEDURE

**Appendix E** . . . . . . . . . . . . . . . . . . . . . . . . . . . . . **219**
    ROOM COMBAT / GENERAL POINTS

**Appendix F** . . . . . . . . . . . . . . . . . . . . . . . . . . . . . **221**
    PREREQUISITES FOR A SUCCESSFUL OPERATION

**NOTES** . . . . . . . . . . . . . . . . . . . . . . . . . . . . . . . . **222**

**"For as we fight—
so must we train."**

# 1.

# THE OVERVIEW

Close Quarter Battle encompasses all the skills required to not only survive a confrontation at close range, but to win and win decisively. These skills range from basic unarmed combat, through combat shooting to advanced team drills. The first parts of this book are devoted to the unarmed aspects of CQB, with the more lethal options in Part IV.

## CQB — UNARMED COMBAT

Before attacking the mechanics of CQB, the reader should have some understanding of the foundation on which most CQB techniques were developed. Although "real world" unarmed combat has little in common with the way fighting is depicted on the silver screen, both find their origins in oriental martial arts. There the similarity ends. Hollywood fight choreographers have selected the techniques that are most visually impressive and tend to prolong the fight scene for dramatic effect. We on the other hand, have selected the most simple and brutal techniques that will bring the confrontation to an end, before it even develops into a fight.

CQB techniques must be easy to learn, simple to perform yet brutally effective. There is nothing nice about a deadly close quarter confrontation.

The oriental masters have long understood the value of repetitive moves to develop reflex action. We have learned the same thing in our modern weapons programs and street survival courses. For a skill to be effectively employed under stress, it must be correctly learned and practiced in training. Officers that have been exposed to sound modern tactical shooting scenarios, have a far greater chance of survival than those that have only shot on a formal bull's-eye type range. Under stress the subconscious can draw on already well learned skills far faster than the conscious mind can recall them. This is known as conditioned response. The same is true for CQB and unarmed combat.

A background in basic martial arts or contact sports, although of some value, will not guarantee survival in the street unless it has been applied to real world scenarios. There are no rules, no referees, and no time limits. Confrontations occur with blinding speed, in darkened areas and often without warning. Your reactions must be reflexive and effective. The only way actions can be reflexive is if they have been correctly taught, completely understood and practiced frequently, in a repetitive, realistic manner.

Although our CQB program has elements of judo, aikido, boxing and street fighting, the foundation can be found in karate. There are many styles of karate, with considerable difference in their techniques, training methods and philosophies. Some encourage the use of soft circular movements, while others put heavy emphasis on the use of the feet. We have found that for techniques to be effective in a CQB role, they must incorporate short hard blows that can be delivered with speed and accuracy, under less than ideal conditions. The style of karate most suited to this role is Shotokan—it is very traditional in concept, but heavily emphasizes hard and fast techniques, repeated until they are reflexive.

This is not to suggest that all black belts in Shotokan Karate are the proverbial lethal weapon. Many a black belt has had his butt kicked in a street confrontation because he did not understand the "rules" of real world street fighting. The first rule being that there are no rules and anything goes. Either that, or he over-estimated his own ability, or under-estimated that of his opponent.

Since balance is so important for not only fighting but also accurate close quarter shooting, we put very little emphasis on kicking techniques except to stamp the last remnants of consciousness out of an adversary. But just as we eliminate the less effective techniques, we never rule out any technique that may fit a specific need. Combat is fast and unpredictable, so the wider the repertoire of techniques that the operator has, the greater his chance of not just survival but victory.

It is not sufficient to simply read this book. The techniques must be studied and repeated literally hundreds of times, until they become as ingrained as any other job related skill.

## THE ROLE OF UNARMED COMBAT IN SPECIAL OPERATIONS

Any student of military history will know that hand-to-hand combat has been an integral part of a warrior's training since the dawn of time. Hand-to-hand combat has proved to be an excellent means of developing self-discipline, physical fitness, agility and controlled aggression in warriors.

*U.S. Marines receive advanced close quarter battle training prior to overseas deployment.*

To this day, many police and military units encourage karate, judo and boxing as part of the training process. One of the prime benefits of martial arts training is the confidence that an individual gains from physically besting another. The individual also comes to realize that there is no place for anger or loss of control. With loss of temper comes irrational actions that can only result in defeat. In the real world, when confronted with physical threat, the individual, confident in his abilities, will show more self-control and be less inclined to over react.

Another character trait lacking in modern man is fighting spirit. It has been many decades since everyday life was a constant fight for survival. Civilization, laws and accepted behavior have suppressed many primal fighting instincts. Before a man can be expected to step into the arena, his fighting spirit must be awakened. Even the gladiators of ancient Rome went through a training process before being matched in mortal combat.

CQB, martial arts and unarmed combat programs serve as an expedient method to awaken the sleeping lion, to gauge a man's willingness to fight, and his ability to control aggression. The fighter must learn to turn this side of himself on and off like a faucet.

It is important that the reader understand that unarmed combat is not the panacea for all problems. There will be times when lethal justice must be dispensed, either in the form of a sniper option or close quarter shooting. CQB, in some areas, has come to mean only the non-lethal forms of fighting, while in the true sense it covers all forms of close quarter battle—both lethal and non-lethal. It will be up to the individual to evaluate the situation and decide what level of force is justified.

Special units tasked with hostage rescue (HRT), have long recognized the need for some form of unarmed combat that could be applied in situations where deadly force was not warranted. It could be in dealing with unarmed criminals, juvenile gang members, to subdue panicked hostages or uncooperative by-standers.

One type of incident that comes to mind is the handling of the families of gang members, while serving felony arrest warrants. Another is counter hijacking situations where the hostages have been in captivity so long that there has developed sympathies for the hostage takers (Stockholm Syndrome). In both cases, unarmed, emotionally distraught, irrational civilians may try to prevent the assault team from securing or shooting the armed terrorists or criminals.

There will also be occasions when a primary weapon may jam or fail to fire, and the assailant is too close to permit the transition to a secondary weapon. The assault team must possess reflexive skills and defensive tactics that will allow them to subdue an attacker, without the use of live fire. Or at least give the time and room to get a failed weapon back into action.

FLEXIBILITY is a key part of all tactical planning that requires a wide variety of options to choose from. The unarmed combat facets of a CQB program will expand and complement the more conventional special weapons skills already possessed by the team.

# SHOOTER BACK-UP

The term "Shooter" has come into popular usage within the special operations community. A shooter is usually the point man, or men, on a SWAT/HRT operation that are most likely to engage the suspects, should lethal force be required. They are usually drawn from the better close quarter combat shooters within the team. It is only logical to select the best man for the job - and some shoot better than others.

In situations where the special operations team is being sent in to subdue "supposedly" unarmed suspects, as in gang houses, civil disturbances and prison riots, the assault team members assigned to engaging the suspects with their bare hands or batons must be backed-up by armed shooters. Armed back-up does not mean the long rifles and snipers that may be deployed for outdoor disturbances. It refers to a buddy system, where each subduer has his own guardian angel in the form of an armed shooter. If the situation escalates, or the suspect pulls a weapons, time and life are not wasted playing the catch-up game.

*Sheriff's Special Weapons Team practices live fire entries during an S.T.T.U. training program*

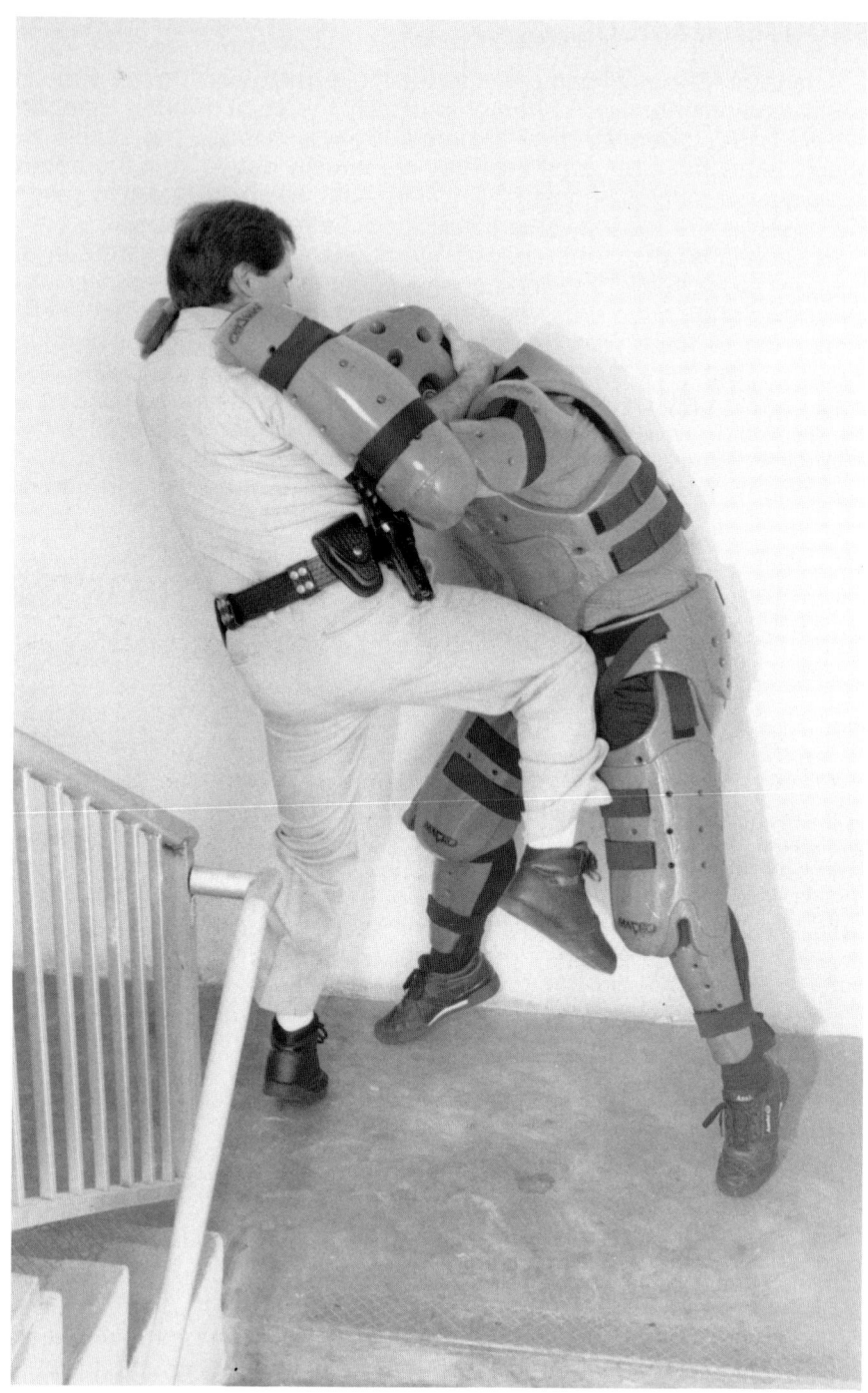

*RedMan protective equipment used for defensive tactics training*

# 2

# TRAINING CONSIDERATIONS

As in any form of training there are certain prerequisites that when met, will greatly expedite the training process. The accompanying photos will illustrate many of the requirements for CQB training, but a few others need to be covered here.

## THE TEAM

All members of a law enforcement or military special operations team should receive CQB training, not just the assault element. Perimeter teams, containment personnel, snipers, command element, communications specialists and medics should all get some grounding in close quarter battle and especially unarmed combat. Although it is the assault element that will have the greatest need for these skills, CQB should be a standard part of all special operations training.

To facilitate training, all team members should possess the following qualities:
- Good physical condition
- Intelligent, stable and mature
- Highly self motivated
- Keen to learn and train
- An individual thinker and a team player

Physical conditioning is an important part of CQB, since the unarmed combat aspects are very physical in nature. Individuals should possess not only strength and endurance, but also speed and flexibility. All team members should be routinely involved in sports or activities that develop stamina and upper body strength. In this way, the time allotted to CQB conditioning can be better used for stretching exercises and muscle specific conditioning.

It is not recommended that a team be sent out for a ten mile run before beginning a CQB class. The team needs to be fresh, rested and alert so that they can learn the new skills without being hampered by fatigue. The CQB training alone is a good work-out, without the need for excessive PT before hand. A simple 10–15 minute warm-up with plenty of stretching exercises will be of more value than a 30 minute burn-out.

*Police Assault Team in training*

*U.S. Navy Seal Team*

## THE INSTRUCTOR

Not all martial arts black belts are good unarmed combat instructors, just as not all pistol champions are good tactical shooting instructors. A CQB instructor should possess the following qualities:
- A sound background in unarmed combat training
- Solid credentials in modern weapons craft
- A good working knowledge of small unit tactics
- Exceptional communication and teaching skills
- The ability to demonstrate what he teaches
- Adequate training aids
- A proven, mission specific training program
- Experience and patience
- The ability to motivate a training team

The instructor must be able to earn the respect of his trainees in the first hours of the program. This will be done through his physical presence, in-depth knowledge, demonstrated ability and willingness to share his experience.

## TRAINING LOCATIONS

CQB training can be divided into three blocks:
1/ Unarmed combat and defensive tactics
2/ Close quarter shooting and room combat
3/ Tactical team scenarios

The unarmed combat can be done almost anywhere, from an open field to the parade ground or gym. It is more beneficial to have a hall or gym set-up for fight training, with punch bags and training mats, but not essential. The key factor being that training can proceed without undue distractions and noise.

The live fire shooting aspects of CQB training will require a shooting range with an assortment of tactical targets and barricades. These are extensively covered in ADVANCED WEAPONS TRAINING for Hostage Rescue Teams.

For realistic training the team will require access to a live-fire shooting house (killing house), that affords multiple room entries and more complex hostage scenarios. If this is not available, a tremendous amount of value can still be derived from some inexpensive plywood walls erected on a conventional range.

## TRAINING EQUIPMENT

The equipment required for CQB training can be divided into two categories: Individual assault equipment and CQB training aids.

Ultimately, CQB should be practiced in full tactical equipment including; entry vests, weapons, gas masks/goggles, gloves, hoods, boots and load-bearing gear. However, in the earlier stages of training it is

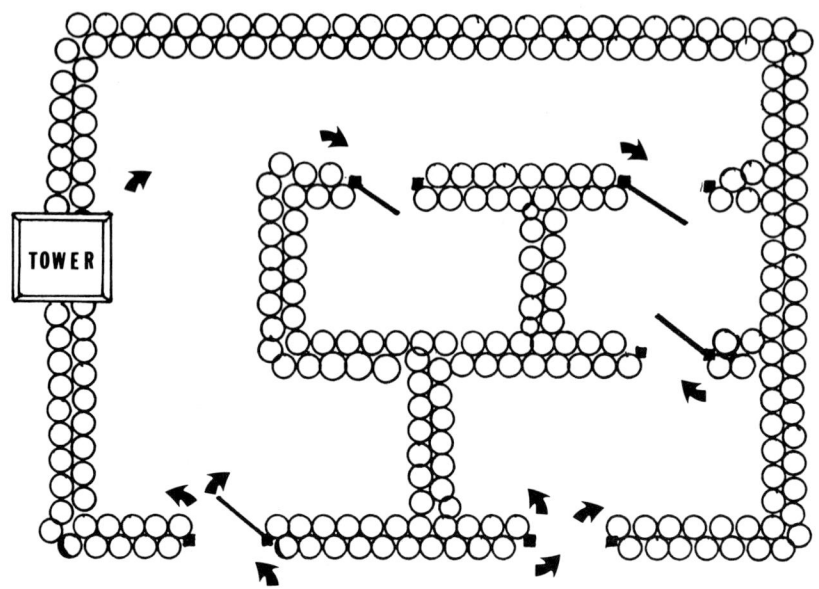

*Plan view of a "killing house"*

*F.B.I. Tire House used for close quarter shooting and hostage rescue*

it is actually more beneficial to the learning process to train in just uniform pants, boots and sweat shirts.

It is important that new skills be learned without the distraction and fatigue caused by excessive equipment. The student will be able to better concentrate on form and technique when he is comfortable and unhindered. But once a new skill is learned, it must be practiced in full kit so that the trainee can experience the limitations brought about by reduced peripheral vision, additional weight and a restricted range of movement.

Unarmed combat training aids consist of an assortment of: punch bags and striking pads; focus mitts; boxing gloves and head protectors; rubber knives and guns; gym mats for falling; and tennis balls to throw at the trainees to develop reflexive dodging skills.

It can also be beneficial to have an assortment of inoperable weapons that the trainees can practice disarming drills with. These weapons will invariably be getting dropped on the floor and damaged as the trainees fight for possession. Old, worn-out or unrepairable firearms are ideal. They can be painted with distinctive markings so as not to be confused with the real thing.

One last piece of equipment should not be over looked in any CQB training - a fully stocked first aid box. Unarmed combat training is very physical and assault team personnel are some what aggressive by nature. There will be numerous cuts, scratches, bangs and bruises that will need administering to. Cold packs and plenty of ice will also go a long way to reducing swelling and returning the man to training without unnecessary delay. Adequate sport tape is also useful for taping up the odd twisted finger or light sprain.

Every effort should be made to keep the trainees under control and minimize the chance of injuries, but unfortunately they are almost inevitable. A combination of the Human Element and Murphy's Law.

*Focus mitt*

*Heavy bag*

*Gloves and head protector for sparring*

*Training bags to help develop speed and power*

*Full contact arrest procedures*

*RedMan protective equipment used in a jail training environment*

## CQB PROGRAM DESIGN

CQB should come in the first phases of a team's basic training. It will normally follow directly after their fundamental weapons training and prior to the more advanced schools such as explosive entry, sniper training, aircraft assault or helicopter deployment.

The ability to go through doors and dominate a room is the foundation of all SWAT/HRT operations. The unarmed combat aspects of CQB will teach a man speed and balance, improving his ability to move with a weapon.

Unarmed combat and close quarter shooting can be taught as separate training modules, but must be ultimately combined for realism. Just as team members learn a variety of individual skills, it is the application of these skills on team drills that is of real value.

A minimum CQB program for a police SWAT team would consist of a 10 day module, where the team does shooting in the morning and spends the afternoons on unarmed combat. If unarmed combat is done first, the trainees' hands and wrists may be too tired and sore to shoot effectively.

The first five days could be devoted to learning fundamental fight skills and brushing up on quick reactive shooting. The second five days would consist of more intense training and practice of these skills under more stressful conditions, e.g., use of full equipment; less cooperative assailants; stronger attacks; live-fire entries; and multiple targets.

Military and national counter terrorist teams should consider 10 days merely a Basic course, and follow it up with a second 10 day Advanced program. There should be sufficient time between programs to give the bruises and scrapes a chance to heal, and the new skills time to sink in. Each program should end with a test to gauge the proficiency of the participants, and the effectiveness of the instructional staff.

All team members will need periodic refresher courses and practice to maintain proficiency in CQB skills. It is only through repetition that these skills can become reflexive. Twice yearly, in-house instructors should go through advanced classes, just to sharpen their skills and to introduce them to new techniques.

# 3

# PRINCIPLES OF UNARMED COMBAT

In an arena as unprincipled as street fighting or unarmed combat, it is hard to imagine that there are any rules of engagement at all. If it can be said that "the first rule is that there are no rules", then we can come up with other principles that may greatly influence the outcome of the confrontation.

The following principles should be taught to, and memorized by all participants in CQB or self defense training:

**1/ FIGHT DIRTY**—There is nothing sporting about unarmed combat, especially when it involves dangerous individuals with criminal intentions. Do not use your bare hands if there is anything at available that could be used as a weapon. Do not hesitate to use an empty or jammed submachine gun or handgun as a striking tool. Bottles, bricks, rocks, bars or boots, etc., can all be used as improvised weapons. Gouge, kick, stamp or even bite if necessary. Show your attacker that you are more at home than he is with street fighting and gutter tactics.

**2/ ATTACK VITAL AREAS**—When confronted with a determined attacker, do not waste time trying to "punch above the belt". We have already said there are no rules so go for the most vulnerable and sensitive areas of the human body. Attack the eyes, throat, groin or any other weak point that presents itself. (See Chapter 5 for more details.)

**3/ ATTACK THE ATTACKER**—Do not be defensive. Nothing surprises an attacker more than to find himself on the receiving end of a crippling attack. An aggressive counter attack can be a winning strategy. Blocking and dodging may be necessary at the start but the sooner you go on the attack, the sooner the confrontation will be over.

**4/ SIMPLICITY OF TECHNIQUE**—Do not confuse techniques that look good with those that work. Keep your counter attacks simple, direct, aggressive and effective. In a fast, close quarter encounter only the simplest of techniques, delivered ruthlessly and with power, can be trusted to get the job done.

**5/ MOMENTUM OF ATTACK**—Seldom will a single blow fell a determined attacker. Your initial counter must be followed-up with a series of effective techniques delivered with controlled aggression, until the attacker is totally subdued. With multiple attackers, one must move quickly from one to the other without giving them time to regroup.

**6/ EXPECT TO GET HURT**—No matter how much training you have had, you must be prepared to absorb some punishment during the assault. The criminal element, gang members, drug dealers or even terrorists are not known to be soft types. It is true that these types seldom possess anything resembling genuine courage or combative skills, but they are often tough and have had some experience in street fighting. Never under estimate your opponent.

**7/ DON'T GO TO THE GROUND WITH AN ATTACKER**—Stay on your feet, maintain balance and mobility. If you go down you will probably be kicked brutally, especially if there are multiple attackers. If your attacker goes down, do not allow him to get back up—use kicks and stamping techniques to finish him off quickly.

**8/ MENTAL PREPARATION**—This involves the mental review of the appropriate defenses against possible attacks. When time is not always available for physical training, one can regularly run various "what if?" scenarios through ones mind. This mental preparation can serve to reinforce good conditioned responses into the subconscious. It also serves to maintain a high level of tactical alertness and combat preparedness.

These eight key principles should be reviewed and recited constantly during the initial phases of CQB / unarmed combat training. Memorize them:

      FIGHT DIRTY
      ATTACK VITAL AREAS
      ATTACK THE ATTACKER
      SIMPLICITY OF TECHNIQUE
      MOMENTUM OF ATTACK
      EXPECT TO GET HURT
      DON'T GO TO THE GROUND
      MENTAL PREPARATION

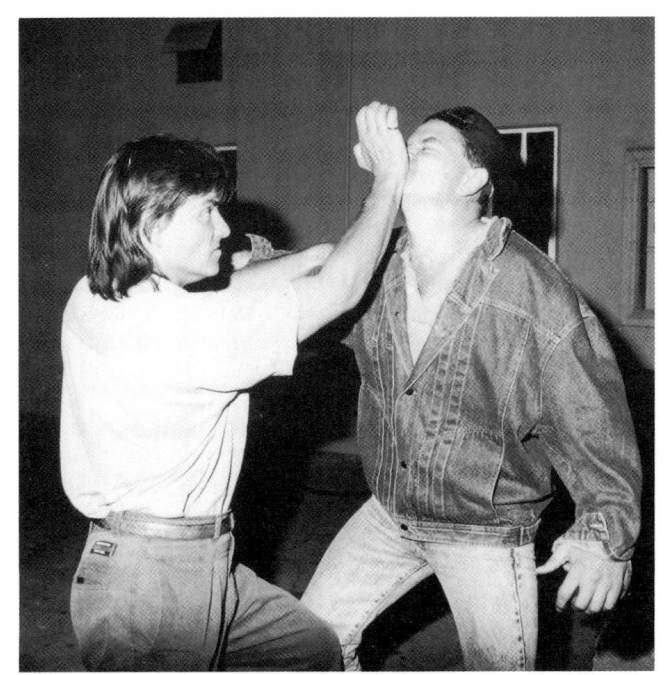
*Strike fast*

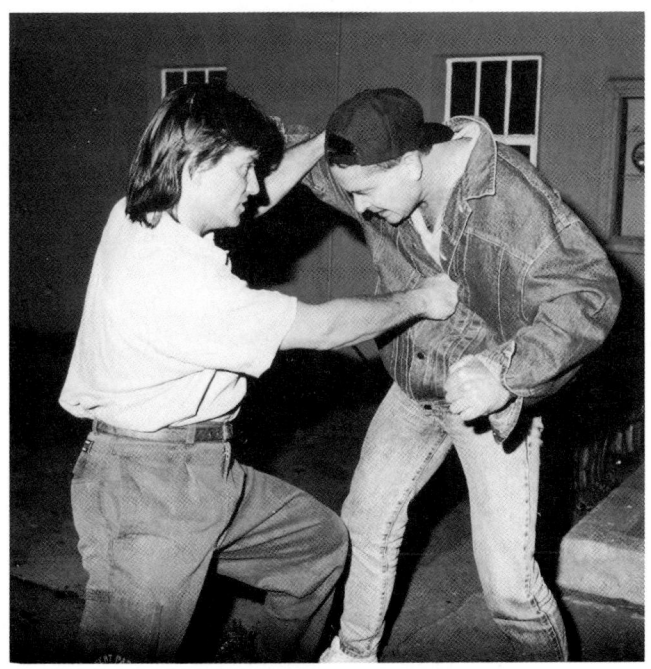
*Strike hard*

# 4.

# MENTAL CONDITIONING FOR SELF DEFENSE

This chapter has been included to assist the CQB instructor, or special operations personnel, who may be tasked with teaching self defense, at some time in his or her career. These classes could be for: patrol officers, investigators, undercover agents, diplomats, military or embassy personnel serving abroad, and the families of all of the above. S.T.T.U.'s STRIKEBACK program was born out of the need for a more generic self defense course for these types of individuals.

The special operations assault team will usually have the benefit of going into a confrontation fore-warned, armed and psyched up for the tasks ahead. Others may be less fortunate and be required to react to a surprise, unprovoked attack where no time is given for mental preparation. Most people's reaction to being threatened or attacked is panic and confusion. So in this chapter we will address some of the general considerations involved in self defense.

There are several steps involved in the mental conditioning of an individual if he or she is to be able to handle a violent confrontation effectively. The first step, and foundation of all others, is acceptance that "it could happen to you". Now that we are in touch with reality, the reality that urban existence can be hazardous to our health, we can begin a process of mental and physical preparation.

Once we accept the realities of violent crime, and that we do not intend being a helpless victim, we must also accept the right to defend ourselves with whatever force is necessary to stop the assault. No-one has the right to touch, hurt or violate another individual, his children or loved ones—and the very thought of such an action should trigger a fierce determination for self preservation. Unfortunately these primal instincts to fight back are often buried by thick layers of "civilized conditioning", to the point that many individuals cannot find the right trigger mechanism, or are afraid to use it. The survival instinct must now be relearned, cultivated, flexed and exercised. This can only be done through realistic and effective self defense programs, where the student is confronted with a wide variety of simulated assaults. Assaults that will trigger all the human responses, including shock, anger, indignation and fear.

Fear is a healthy defense mechanism built into the human psyche which can save us from injury, especially when confronted with activities or incidents beyond our abilities. A classic example would be the fear of approaching the edge of a cliff and therefore avoiding the possibility of falling. From a self defense viewpoint, this could be equated to staying away from rough neighborhoods and low-life bars, there by avoiding a nasty confrontation. Unfortunately fear can have both a positive and a negative effect on human performance. Fear can help us to avoid danger or supply us the added strength/adrenal rush to fight for our lives. On the negative side, fear has the ability to totally paralyze an individual, causing panic and confusion in the face of imminent danger. The increased pulse-rate, the nervous tension, the tightening chest, the hot flush, and the acute awareness are all indicators that increased adrenalin output is taking affect and the body is going into the "fight or flight" mode. Under these conditions the human body is capable of great feats of speed and strength—as long as one does not freeze in fear.

To overcome, or at least control fear (primarily of the unknown), avoid panic and react effectively, we must understand more about how assaults occur and how best to defend oneself. The whole self defense process is more than just learning some fancy moves. It includes the study of actual assaults, the counter attacks, and then realistic simulations. When the student begins to recognize some of the common points in the assaults, and realizes that he or she has the power and ability to disable the attacker(s), a new confidence and strength is born from within.

Anger is another emotion that can have either a positive or negative effect on one's performance. It can cause blind illogical behavior or, on the up side, it can add power and determination to a counter-attack. A potential rape victim has every right to experience fear and anger when assaulted. But these two strong emotions must be harnessed into righteous indignation and fierce determination, and then coupled to a crippling counter-attack-commonly known as controlled aggression.

Individuals not accustomed to dealing with violence can be frozen into inactivity by the surprise of the initial assault. This must be immediately countered by some positive, assertive action that will trigger the more physical defense mechanisms. In the more progressive self defense programs taught throughout the United States, the students are conditioned to shout "NO!" in a very strong, authoritative voice as the prelude for defensive/offensive moves. Once the decision to fight back has been made the victim must become the aggressor. The counter-attack must be swift, violent and effective.

*Simulated attacks will help to overcome fear that may otherwise paralyze the victim.*

This controlled aggression or violent counter-attack does not come easy for many people, especially women who have been conditioned by society to be caring, loving and gentle by nature. It is not unusual to have a female self defense student that believes she is incapable of the aggressive techniques required of her. For example; eye gouging, groin kicking and head stamping. The student may go so far as to worry about the attacker's safety and well being. At this point, it is up to the instructional staff to graphically explain to the student what could happen if she does not fight back; to document the brutal assaults on other women; and then expose her to several simulated attacks, with class and staff encouragement. For patrol officers it is simply a matter of studying the number and types of attacks on police officers throughout the U.S.

The instructors, who role-play as "attackers" in the self defense program, must be schooled to imitate, verbally and physically, actual attackers as much as possible within the training structure. These "attackers", when fitted with protective gear, must also be taught to react realistically to the counter-attacks launched by students. In this manner, the student is exposed to the crude language and violent behavior that will accompany the assault, and not be frozen with shocking by the real thing. In addition, the student will experience the confidence that comes with not only surviving but winning.

Role playing and simulated assaults will teach the students to evaluate the attacker and seek out the most advantageous time to launch a counter-attack. Perhaps when the rapist is distracted or fumbling with his pants, or when the mugger reaches for your wallet or purse. The whole role playing process is to take the mystery, and with it some of the fear, out of street violence. Remember, it is the unknown that we fear most.

After a little training the students must be taught mental rehearsal of theoretical attacks and counter-attacks. These are what we call the "What ifs . . . ?" All law enforcement officers should be taught to use the same technique. As they patrol the streets, approach a disturbance or enter a suspect location they should run a series of "what ifs . . . ?" through their conscious thought process. This could consist of: "What if someone is waiting around this next corner . . .?" "What if he goes for a weapon as I approach him . . . ?" "What if I am walking into a setup . . . ?" "What if I hear gun shots . . . ?" — These are mentally answered by plans to go for cover; draw a weapon; return fire; retreat; call for assistance; etc.

Other individuals can do the same thing as they go jogging in the park; pass a group of rough punks on the street; find themselves in the sub-way with a suspicious individual; enter a parking garage; hear a noise in the house at night. By consciously rehearsing your contingency plans, to escape, call 911 or fight, you are conditioning the subconscious to react correctly under stress. When and if the assault comes, you are already one step ahead of the attacker. This is not a sense of paranoia but more a common sense approach to urban survival.

With the decision to fight one must also accept a degree of pain and the possibility of injury. This is especially true when knives, broken bottles and sharp instruments are involved. The probability of getting cut is very real. Even in a confrontation where no weapons are involved there will still be bruises, scrapes and falls. Shock, anger, fear and adrenalin will mask much of the discomfort. Pain must be blocked from conscious thought by counter-attacking with vigor and determination. A little pain, while fighting off the assault, is preferable to the permanent physical and psychological injuries, or even death, that accompanies many rapes and beatings.

With the acceptance of reality and some effective training comes a new confidence and awareness. The student is more capable of identifying and avoiding potential trouble spots. Recognizing the pre-indicators of an assault may give the individual time to escape, seek assistance or better prepare for the confrontation. If the assault comes as a total surprise the victim will have well ingrained conditioned responses that should kick-in automatically without the need for the slower conscious thought processes. During the fight the potential victim will become the aggressor, with a small but effective repertoire of crippling counter-attacks, blocks, strikes, kicks and throws.

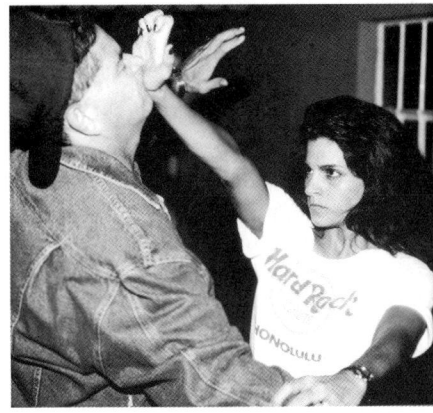

*Determination and a fierce counter-attack*

**Key striking points**

# 5.
# HUMAN ANATOMY

To be an effective fighter, one must know not only how to deliver a powerful blow but also where to land it for maximum effect. The human body is an articulated frame work of bone, held together by sinew and muscle, surrounding and supporting a system of vital organs, and often protected by layers of fat. Some bones break more easily than others, while some are more structurally important. Just as some organs are more important (vital) than others, and some are more sensitive (vulnerable) to blows.

To clarify terminology, there is a difference between vital and vulnerable areas. The true meaning of the word vital is "that which is essential to life". In CQB it can be considered any area of the body that when struck with sufficient force will immediately incapacitate an assailant. A vulnerable area may not be a vital area but simply a good "target of opportunity", or any area of the body that can be struck or broken to contribute to an attackers eventual defeat.

There are several ways to win a close quarter confrontation. Obviously shooting an attacker in the head or heart will usually (but not always) guarantee fairly swift and deadly results. This will be covered in more detail in Part IV which addresses close quarter shooting. For now we will concentrate on the ability to incapacitate a villain with our bare hands, feet or any other part of the body that we can utilize as a weapon.

The object of the exercise is to deliver a crippling blow, or series of blows, that will stop the attacker in the shortest possible time, and not necessarily with the most physical damage. The priority is not on killing or maiming the attacker, but on STOPPING his threatening action(s). In the process of stopping this miscreant, it may be necessary to severely injure or kill him, but that is not the initial intention, usually.

There are several ways to incapacitate a human being. One can attack components of the nervous system such as the brain or spine; the circulatory system that carries oxygenated blood to the body and brain; the respiratory system which includes the lungs, throat and wind pipe; or the skeletal system by breaking essential bones. For maximum effect, the CQB philosophy is to attack several of these areas systematically and simultaneously.

The above paragraph may give the reader the impression that the human body is very delicate and vulnerable to attack. This is both true and also quite far from the truth. Under ideal conditions, one could incapacitate another human being quite easily, but a determined attacker is not going to be an easy "push-over". Man (the species) has been blessed with certain skills and attributes for self preservation. These include: a functional and resourceful brain; strong bones that protect vital areas; strong, resilient muscle tissue; deposits of fatty padding; quick reflexes, agility and balance; and a sensory system to detect danger. One only has to watch two prize fighters slugging it out for fifteen rounds, to realize the amount of punishment that the human body can absorb, if it is well conditioned.

Conditioning and training are two key considerations when evaluating an opponents survivability in a toe-to-toe confrontation. After a good unarmed combat program, a special operations team member should be well equipped to handle most situations. On the dark side, your opponent has probably grown up on the streets, and already survived years in a criminal environment with some very tough characters. Add to this his post-graduate training received in the Federal or State

**Eyes and throat are both key targets.**

prison system—'The University of Folsom' or similar institution. Two to ten years pumping iron in a well equipped, State supplied "iron pit"; surviving gang and race conflicts in the general prison population; and comparing techniques with other inmates, can create quite a tough adversary.

CQB training should teach not only where and how to hit, but also how to read an opponent and create opportunities to attack vital areas. The following chapters will illustrate how best to attack these key anatomical areas.

**VITAL & VULNERABLE AREAS**

The eyes, throat and groin are the softest targets and the ones we are most often taught to attack. These are excellent targets but they are also the ones most protected by a street smart fighter. The spec-ops trainee needs a little more in-depth understanding of the vital areas to give him increased flexibility in his attacks. Attacking these vital areas will allow him to maximize the pain inflicted upon his opponent with a minimum energy expenditure. Extreme pain alone, without permanent injury, can often be sufficient to deter or render an attacker helpless.

**THE HEAD:**
    a. eyes
    b. temples
    c. nose
    d  jaw
    e. ears
    f. throat
    g. base of skull

If an attacker cannot see, it is difficult for him to pursue the attack. Blows to the nose and jaw can cause severe pain and disorientation. Blows to the base of the skull and temples can cause unconsciousness or death. A cupped blow to the ears can rupture the ear drums causing severe pain and loss of balance. Strikes to the throat can result in choking, unconsciousness or death.

**THE TORSO:**
    a. collar bone
    b. sternum
    c. ribs
    d. solar plexus
    e. stomach
    f. kidneys
    g. groin
    h. spine

When fighting a determined attacker there are no 100% guarantees that any single blow will do the job. His mental attitude and physical condition may greatly lessen the effect of blows delivered to the torso in particular. Assailants with heavy bones and considerable muscularity in the upper body may be very difficult to injure with conventional punches to the chest, stomach or shoulders. However there are three areas that are vulnerable: the throat, the solar plexus and the groin.

**THE LIMBS:**
    a. All joints;
       shoulders
       elbows
       wrists
       fingers
       knees
       ankles
    b. thighs
    c. shins
    d. instep

Bones and joints are not considered vital areas in the life threatening sense, but breaking these vulnerable areas will often take all the fight out of an attacker. Injury to joints, like the elbow or knee, will serve to immobilize an attacker and deny use of that limb, even if it does not totally incapacitate him.

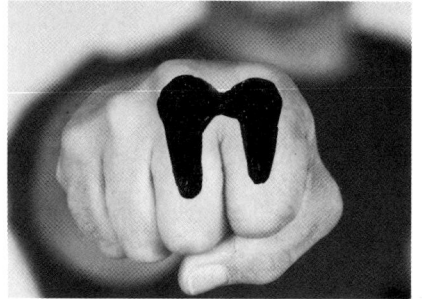

*Horizontal punch*

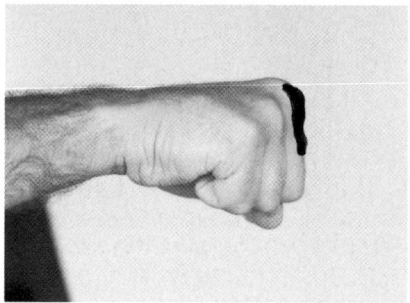

*Horizontal punch*

*Vertical punch*

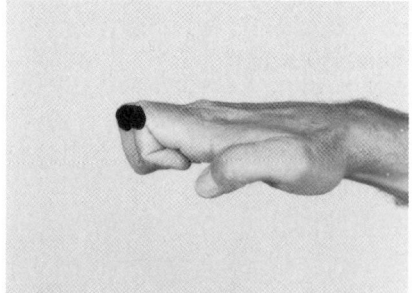

*Quarter punch*

# NATURAL WEAPONS OF THE HUMAN BODY

Contrary to popular belief, not every red-blooded male can ball his hand into the perfect fist and deliver a jaw breaking punch. In fact, without formal boxing or karate training, very few can. It is not uncommon for unskilled street fighters to break their hands on the harder parts of their opponents body.

It is also well known in CQB circles that the fist is not always the ideal striking implement. If a situation may escalate into gun play then one does not want to be breaking knuckles or damaging one's shooting hand. In addition, select vital areas of the human body are better struck with an open hand of one form or another. Two examples would be the fingers to the eyes and the cupped hand to the ears.

The following is a list of the natural weapons of the human body, and where best to direct them:

**FIST**—strikes to the jaw, head, ribs, solar plexus, stomach, kidneys, base of skull, etc
**HAMMER FIST**—strikes to the temples, solar plexus, base of skull, ribs, forearm and elbow
**PALM HEEL**—strikes to the base of the nose, upper lip, side of the jaw, under the chin, temple and elbow
**FINGERS**—to the eyes or throat
**CUPPED HAND**—to the ears
**QUARTER FIST**—to the throat
**WEB HAND**—to the throat
**RIDGE HAND**—to neck, groin or solar plexus
**ELBOW**—to the head and upper body
**KNEE**—to the groin, lower stomach and thighs
**TOES**—straight kicks to knees or groin, or the head of a downed opponent
**HEEL**—stamping kicks to the instep of a standing opponent, or to the chest, head or thigh of a downed opponent
**HEAD**—strikes to the soft facial area at close range

A series of effective strikes to vulnerable areas of your opponents body will give better results than a prolonged tussle. However, there is a word of warning. It can prove quite damaging to the operator if he lashes out at an assailant wearing load-bearing equipment and protective gear. Strikes against loaded magazine pouches, weapons, ballistic plates and helmets, may only serve to break bones in the hand, wrist or elbow. If blows cannot be placed accurately, then alternatives must be explored.

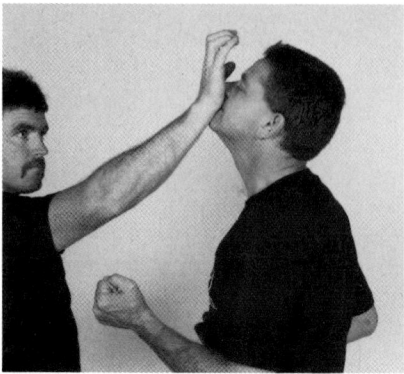

*Palm-heel strike*

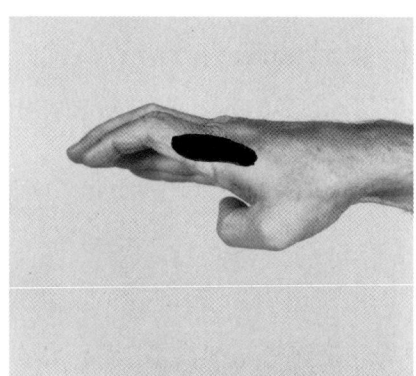
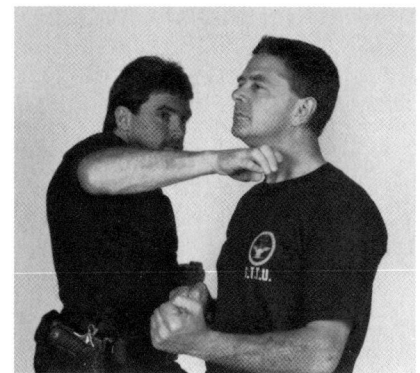

*Ridge hand strike*

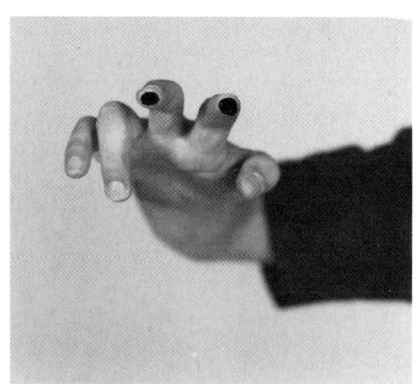

*Web hand*        *Fingers to eyes*

*Palm-heel strike used to drive the head into the deck*

*Cupped hand strike to the ear*

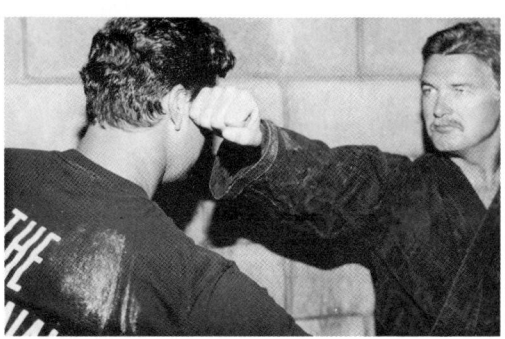

*Four applications of the hammer punch*

# PART II

# UNARMED COMBAT

*Solid fighting stance*

*Hammer punch to the solar plexus from straddle stance*

# 6

# FIGHTING FUNDAMENTALS

Before progressing to the actual offensive and defensive techniques involved in the STTU CQB program, the trainee must understand the fundamental principles of balance and movement, as they relate to close quarter combat.

One of the laws of physics tells us "that for every action there is an equal and opposite reaction". In fight terms, this means that the when striking an attacker, the power generated by a punch is delivered equally into the target as it is back into one's fist. Therefore one must be able to structurally absorb an equal amount of energy as the victim. If not, this may result in loss of balance, decreased power or a broken hand.

Speed, power and accuracy are also critical factors in close quarter battle. If a technique is not performed quickly (reflexively) then the element of surprise will be lost. The fighter must have sufficient strength, and the technique sufficient force, to do serious damage to the assailant or the confrontation will only be prolonged. Lastly, the strikes and breaks must be delivered with some accuracy to hit vulnerable areas and to take advantage of exposed vital points.

## STANCES

The foundation of all fighting is the stance. The correct stance gives strength, power, balance and agility to the fighter. It should be a natural posture; be equally effective for either defensive or offensive techniques; be quick and easy to assume; and yet still permit rapid changes of direction.

We have reduced the number of formal karate stances down to three essential positions:
- the basic stance
- the forward fighting stance (left or right)
- the straddle stance

These three stances supply all the essentials of balance, strength and flexibility. (see photos)

*Horizontal lunge punch*

*Horizontal reverse punch*

*Rising block*        *Vertical punch*

## BALANCE

It requires no special training to maintain balance while standing still, but when involved in the dynamics of mortal combat, it can be considerably more challenging. The fighter must be able to maintain balance and control through a wide range of motions including advancing, retreating, side stepping, turning, dodging, ducking, kicking and maneuvering around obstacles. This is best achieved by keeping a wide, stable base and your center of gravity low.

Crisis entry and room combat brings the operator into contact with a wide variety of building designs, furniture, stairs and barricades—all of which must be negotiated while rescuing hostages and engaging hostage takers. There is nothing quite as embarrassing as falling over your own size 11s during a training exercise—or as fatal on a real operation. The principles of balance and movement taught in CQB, or any martial art, will be of tremendous value to a shooter, especially in the close confines of a residential dwelling, bus or plane.

## MOVEMENT

A necessary extension of stance and balance is movement. But one cannot sacrifice balance for movement. Most "black role" special operations involve assaulting a stronghold or barricade location, for the purpose of suspect apprehension or hostage rescue. That is not the time to be losing control, tripping or falling.

Some basic principles of movement are:
- Do not wear clothing or equipment that will hinder movement
- Select your footwear carefully
- Keep your weapon pointed forward / towards the threat
- Study the terrain before moving
- Be aware of available cover
- Stay alert
- Place your feet carefully
- Maintain balance
- Avoid crossing your feet in confined areas
- Do not run unless you have to
- Consider noise discipline
- Avoid going prone in tactical situations that require mobility

Practice, practice and more practice is the remedy to all movement problems. Remember, the only difference between training and the real thing, is that when its for real, you don't get any more mistakes.

# 7.

# STRIKES & BLOCKS

Although it is recognized that the legs are stronger than the arms, and a kick is usually more damaging than a punch, there are many instances in CQB where it is ill advised to sacrifice one's balance by attempting to kick. To be a competent fighter, one must develop a few effective punches and strikes.

Over the years we have learned two things about punching. Firstly, no one is born with the ability to punch well. Secondly, any one can be taught to strike effectively, immaterial of size, weight or sex. Our "average male" will usually break his hand or simply fail to have any effect when he lashes out at a determined attacker. When the decision to strike has been made, the attack must be launched with crippling effectiveness. Lashing out ineffectively may only serve to enrage the attacker and result in additional injury to yourself.

There is far more to striking than simply knowing how to make a fist. In fact, in many strikes we do not use a fist at all, preferring to opt for an open-hand technique. For a strike to be effective it must have **speed**, **power**, **accuracy** and **surprise**. This is in addition to being technically correct in terms of molding the hand into a striking implement.

## STRIKES

The basic hand strikes that we prefer are the palm-heel strike, the hammer fist, the horizontal punch, and the vertical punch, with some variations on each. Each striking technique , as seen in the photos, is designed to meet a specific need in reaction to different attacks. All techniques should be practiced both left and right handed.

The **palm-heel** strike is an open-hand technique that is usually targeted at the upper lip or just beneath the nose. It is a very effective upward driving blow that can be used to cripple or simply to break contact with the attacker. After driving the head back, because of severe pain to the nose, the assailants throat is left wide open for follow-up attacks, as is the groin and solar plexus.

The **hammer punch** is a closed fist technique which is usually employed as a horizontal blow to the sternum or a down-ward blow to the head or neck. The hammer punch is a powerful technique that can also be used to break grips or strike any unprotected part of the body.

The **horizontal and vertical punches** are directly related and most resemble the conventional punches we are used to seeing on TV. The selected vital area and the distance to that area will dictate which punch is utilized. Horizontal punches when one requires full reach and vertical punches for closer in fighting. It is essential that the CQB trainee carefully study the correct formation of the fist before attempting punches on any of the training bags. An incorrect punch can result in painful injuries to the knuckles and wrist.

It is not uncommon for street brawlers and untrained fighters to sustain broken fingers and knuckles as a direct result of poor technique and incorrect fist formation. Remember that boxers carefully tape their hands before donning gloves, not only to protect the opponent but also the fighters' hands. It is important that the fist be in-line with the wrist and that only the first two knuckles be employed as the primary striking surface. In martial arts classes, the students first master the fist formation, then move onto light strikes against a pad or focus mitt. Only once the instructor is satisfied with the form will the student move onto to developing power against the heavier punch bags.

*Palm-heel strike*

*Horizontal punch*

 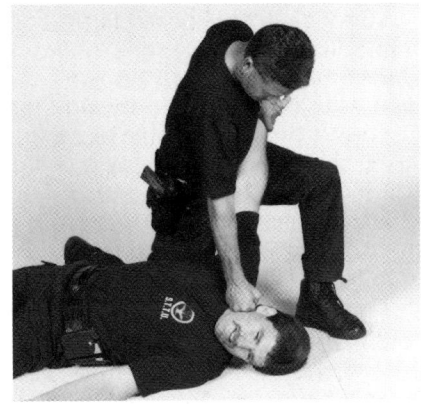

*Vertical punches*

*Cupped hand*        *Quarter punch*

There is less chance of knuckle breakage with the palm-heel strike and hammer punch, so those are usually taught first. Other open-hand techniques that ares easy to learn and extremely effective are: the cupped hand; the quarter punch; two finger thrust; ridge hand strike; and the web hand strike.

The **cupped hand** (also known as the slap hand) is directed against the ears, either singularly or simultaneously. This cupped slapping technique causes a pocket of air to be compressed into the ear and results in a burst ear-drum, severe pain, disorientation and loss of balance. In some cases the pain is sufficient to cause unconsciousness.

The **quarter punch** is a half fist (where the first two knuckles are rolled in but not the entire fist) that also requires considerable training to master, but is very effective against soft targets such as the throat and groin. (See photos)

The **two finger** thrust is targeted against the eyes and is one of the most effective techniques when performed correctly and with conviction. The hand is locked into a semi-curved claw and thrust directly into the face with the first and second fingers going into the eye sockets.

The **ridge hand strike** is performed with one of the few semi-circular motions utilized in our style of fighting, and is used to lash out at the sides of the head and neck. It can also be used effectively in the form of an up-ward arc into the groin, from below the attackers peripheral vision. From the side the ridge hand can be looped into the solar plexus or bridge of the nose.

The **web hand strike** is achieved by spreading the thumb and index finger, tightening the web of the hand and then driving it horizontally into the throat. When done with sufficient force it can cause severe damage to the wind pipe, choking, unconsciousness and even death. After the strike the hand need not be withdrawn, and can be used to grip onto the throat in a choking hold.

The final addition to our list of strikes is the family of elbow strikes and **forearm smashes**. The elbow strikes are usually performed when an assailant is behind and very close. The forearm techniques are best utilized against an attacker who is very close and directly in front. (See photos)

To bring everything back into perspective, none of the strikes are effective unless accompanied by the four elements—speed, power, accuracy and surprise.

**SPEED**—An attacker will block or stop a counter punch if he sees it coming and has time to react. A half hearted technique, a faint or one that lacks determination will only serve to warn your attacker that you intend to resist. The counter attack must be fast, effective and continuous until the attacker is beaten.

**POWER**—It is not necessary to have the arms of the Hulk or the training of Mike Tyson to be able to put power into a punch or strike. The strength in your arms is only a small part of the power behind a good punch. The bulk of the power will be drawn from the shoulders, back, legs and body rotation.

As with any counter attack you will need to close distance with your assailant—attack the attacker! The very motion of lunging forward will add both body weight and leg power to your strike.

The shorter, closer strikes will draw more power from the arms and shoulders so develop these areas by concentrating on shoulder and triceps exercises in the gym.

**ACCURACY**—The human body has a tremendous capability to absorb punishment, but there are areas that can not withstand even a moderately powered blow. To rain blows on your assailants back, chest, shoulders, upper arms and thighs may only serve to tire yourself and enrage him. Wait, pick your time, pick your target and attack with conviction. The eyes, throat and groin are all excellent targets to begin with—fight dirty! In addition, attacks to the ears, nose, temples, solar plexus and heart can prove very effective.

**SURPRISE**—The element of surprise has been a winner in battles since the dawn of time. The attacker who is used to intimidating his victims may be a cowardly bully at heart who gets his rocks off by targeting the weak. When you pick your time and explode into action with potentially crippling counter attacks, he may well be surprised into fleeing if not dropped by your initial strikes. Once you initiate your defense give no quarter, show a fierce determination to win and attack with a calculating controlled aggression.

Only on the rarest occasions will one punch or strike end a confrontation. A trained Black Belt or professional boxer may be able place his best shot with sufficient power to incapacitate an assailant, but the average person will need to follow-up the initial counter-attack with two or three other strikes. The general rule is to continue the attack until the assailant is no longer a danger to you and a retreat can be made safely.

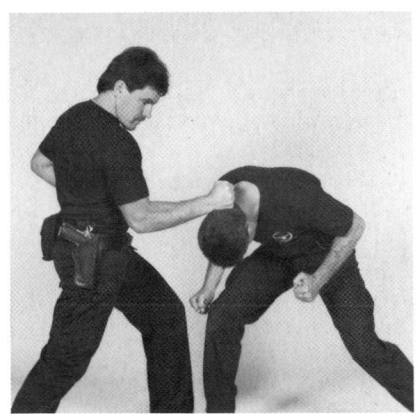
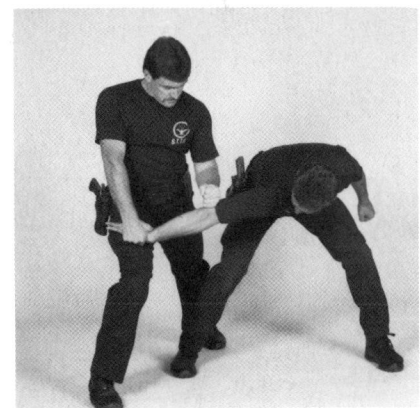

*Various hammer punches*

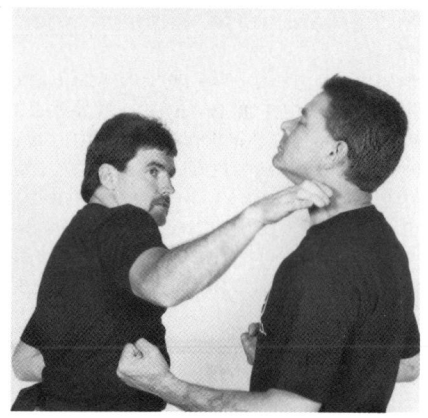
**Web hand**

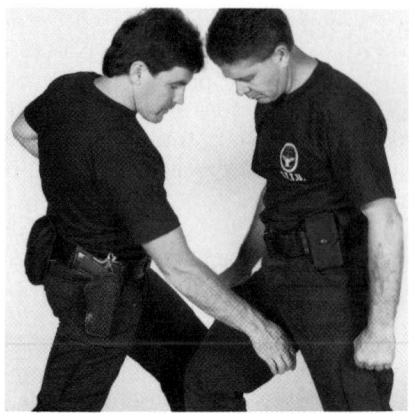
**Ridge hand**

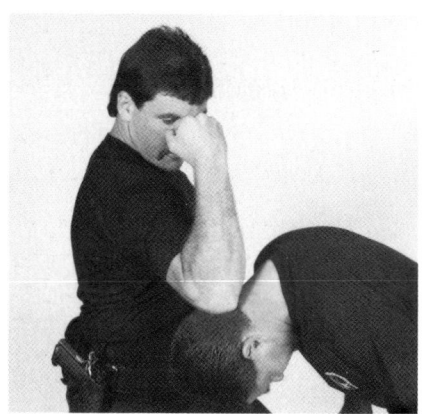
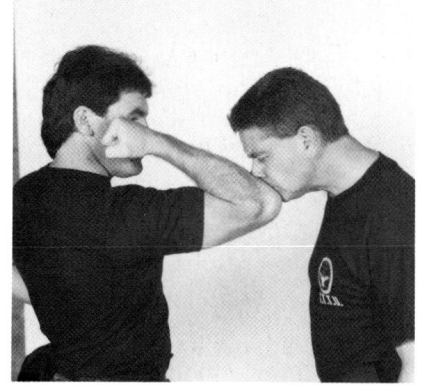
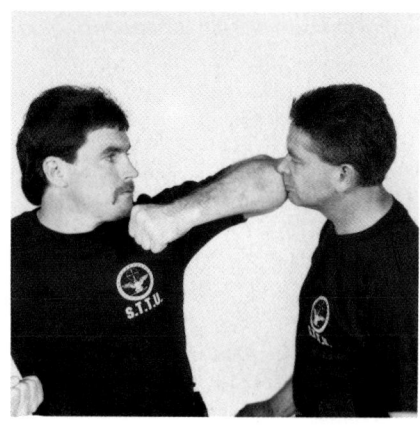

**Elbow and forearm strikes**

## BLOCKS

An equally important aspect of learning to strike is learning to block strikes that are directed against you. The block is often the first line of defense against an act of aggression, so must therefore be a reflexive, conditioned response. The blocking action must be fast, accurate and positive.

The key basic blocks in the STTU-CQB program are:
- the downward block
- the rising block
- the cross block
- the pressing block

The **downward block** is used primarily to deflect low thrusting attacks and kicks to the stomach and groin.

The **rising block** to protect against downward knife or club strikes or punches to the face.

The **cross block** can also be used for punches or thrusts to the face, throat or high chest, and to deflect attempts to grab the front of your uniform. The cross block can be performed from the outside inward or the inside outward.

The **pressing block** is softer, open hand form of the cross block that is fast and effective when trying to deflect an attack to the head or throat.

With all blocks, it is essential that the trainee be flexible, ready to move and ready to counter punch. Blocks should be practiced left and right handed, to defend against attacks from either side. Should the blocking technique be less than ideal, a body shift will prevent the attacker's blow from landing on its intended target. Shuffling to the right and left, backwards and forwards should be incorporated into the more advanced blocking drills.

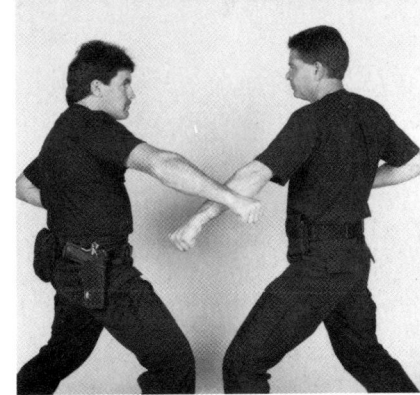

*Downward block*

The block is only the first phase of the defense. Phase 2 is to turn the defense into the offense. ATTACK THE ATTACKER. To prepare for this, as the block is initiated, the other hand is immediately cocked to strike. Then as each strike is fired off, the other hand recocks to follow up the counter attack.

Trainees should be introduced to blocking slowly. Initial man-on-man drills will produce some nasty bruises on the forearms, as bone meets bone. It may be necessary to caution the more enthusiastic trainees about the use of excessive force on their own team mates.

***Inside cross block***

***Outside cross block***

***Pressing block***

*Rising block*

*Bunt/deflection*

## BASIC SPARRING

Once strikes and blocks have been perfected, the students need to begin developing a feel for **distance**. The distance between themselves and an attacker. The distance at which different techniques can be applied. They must learn the small, shuffling quarter steps that are used to close distance and evade attacks, without loss of balance.

In basic sparring, the two trainees face each other from a fixed distance and take turns attacking and defending. In each drill the mode of attack and intended target are **predetermined**.

The next step is semi-free one blow sparring. Both attacker and defender assume a relaxed ready position while moving about. The attacker must find an opening while seeking the proper distance from his opponent from which to launch the attack. The defender must watch for the attack and be ready to defend, with an appropriate block and counter attack.

All punches, strikes and kicks must be **"pulled"** just short of contact. This is to develop control, accuracy and discipline. Only when this ability to pull punches has been developed, should the students be permitted to don gloves and protective equipment, and indulge in free sparring.

The heavy entry vest and body armor, without the rigid inserts, are excellent upper body protection for sparring. However, the head and hands should still be protected with boxing helmets and gloves. A groin guard, shin and forearm guards and a mouth piece are also recommended if full contact sparring is on the schedule.

Final point. Controlled aggression and fighting spirit are commendable characteristics for a modern-day warrior, but the emphasis is very much on control. Sparring sessions must be carefully monitored by the instructor to prevent situations getting out of hand. Participants that cannot control their temper or enthusiasm have no place on a high-speed team that is required to perform surgical operations. That same loss of control is a liability exposure that could escalate into an excessive force charge, or even unjustified homicide.

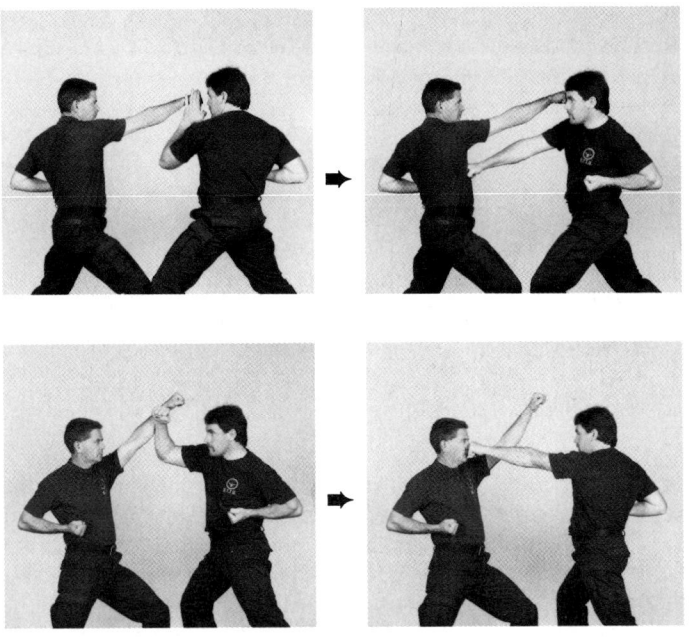

*Basic sparring*

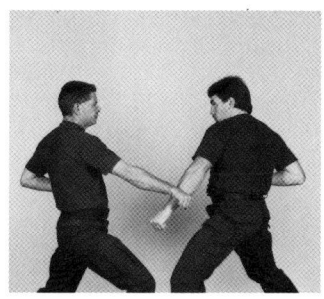 

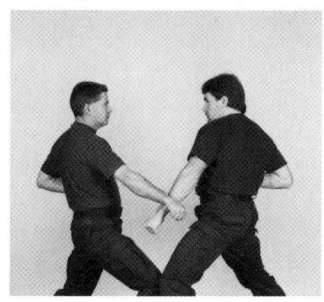 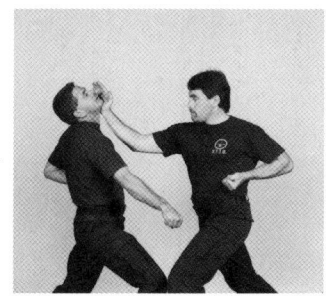

*Basic sparring*

*Basic sparring*

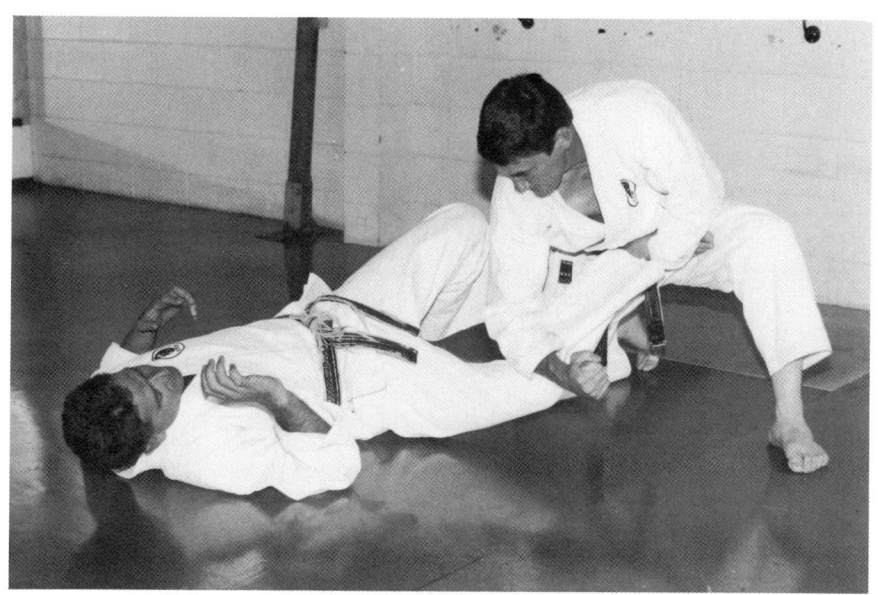

*Advanced sparring can be extended to take-downs and follow-up techniques.*

*Back-fist to groin*

*Full side kick*

**The danger of high kicks in the "real world"**

# 8.

# KICKS

In the previous chapter on striking we stated that when attempting to kick in a confined area we may be sacrificing balance. Never the less, kicking is an important part of CQB. This is quite logical since the leg muscles are considerably stronger than the arms and are therefore capable of inflicting more damage. Add to that the fact that a good pair of boots will not only protect the feet, they can become an effective improvised weapon.

Another reason for developing effective kicking techniques is the that the assault team members will always have some form of weapon in their hands. Kicking allows one to strike-out without releasing the grip on the weapon.

The first step towards developing kicks as an effective offensive/defensive tool, is to realize that the high-flying spinning round-house kicks seen in various kung-fu movies have no place in a down and dirty street fight. A martial arts expert or PKA kick-boxer, with years of training, may be able to make one of these flashy high kicks work. But most would opt for a lower, faster more devastating technique when their life depended on it.

When trying to high kick to the head, the foot has considerably more distance to travel than if directed to the knee or groin. This "time in air" gives your opponent more time to see it coming and more time to react. You also expose your groin, sacrifice your balance and risk having your leg caught in mid-air—a nasty situation at best...

Once all the flashy martial arts kicks have been eliminated, we are left with a small but effective repertoire of usable kicks. These are divided into two categories: kicks with the foot which can be used at medium to close range; and kicks with the knee which we will look at first. The knee to the groin is probably the one that people are most familiar with and is still a valid technique. It is also the counter-attack most expected and unfortunately defended against.

The technique is very simple. One simply drives the knee upward into the groin of an attacker when he comes close enough (usually twice). It can also be used in the prone position if an attacker is lying on top or under you. The difficult part of this technique is the timing. It must be executed with speed and power, when the attacker least expects it. The optimum timing being as the attacker's hands and mind are occupied, or following a distracting blow to his face.

After a blow to the stomach or groin an injured attacker will tend to bend forward at the waist. This is a good time to grasp his hair or head and deliver follow-up knee strikes to the face, head or chest. The most common mistake made during training is to attempt a knee to the groin prematurely or without conviction. It is then easily deflected by raising the thigh or rotating the hips.

The primary foot kicks are the stamping kick, the front kick (two variations), the side kick and the axe kick—each with its own advantages and applications.

The **stamping kick** is utilized in two situations. The first when grabbed from behind, the victim can stamp down onto the attacker's foot to create pain and aid in escaping the grip. If done with a boot or hard soled shoe it will have considerable effect and disable an attacker, temporarily. The second place the stamp kick can be utilized, is when the attacker is already down and the operator has the opportunity to stamp down onto the villain's head, or any other available body part.

The **front kick** is practiced in two forms; a straight kick where the foot is picked up and then delivered directly to the knee or groin and a rising kick which is slapped up directly between the attacker's legs. Again the groin kick is an expected attack so must be delivered with speed and surprise. Kicks to the knee cap are less expected, harder to stop and equally effective. An attacker with a broken or dislocated knee will have considerable trouble continuing the attack, or even remaining standing.

The **side kick** is usually delivered to the side or back of the knee, or to the head or throat of an already downed attacker. The side kick utilizes the outer edge of the foot and is more effective when combined with a boot or hard soled shoe.

The **axe kick** is a real power move and fight stopper but can only be used as a coup-de-grace to finish a downed attacker. The axe kick utilizes the heal of the foot and is delivered with all the speed and power that the trainee can muster (see photos).

When training for any of these kicks the student must first warm-up, stretch-out and then **concentrate on maintaining balance** while kicking. The danger with kicks is that one is sacrificing some balance for the speed and power of the technique. Once the student has mastered the move, the instructor should have the student kick at various striking bags with increasing force. After delivering the kick the student must immediately return to full balance and decide how to follow-up with additional attacks.

**Knee strikes**

**Front kick**      **Side kick**

**Stamping side kick**      **Stamping kick**

**Axe kick**

The next step in a realistic training program is to attempt these kicks in full SWAT gear. Most initial training is done wearing sweats that give more freedom of movement than boots, entry vest and weapons load. A vest that is low in the front or has an integral groin protector, will hinder movement and make it more difficult to raise the leg high enough to kick. Heavy combat boots also have a different feel to light weight running shoes.

The novice must not be squeamish about "putting the boot in" and kicking once the attacker is down. Sporting behavior such as allowing the attacker to get back up is absolutely suicidal. The counter attack must continue until the attacker is no longer a threat. This will often mean kicking until the attacker is unconscious or incapacitated. Do not be fooled by the cowardly attacker that fakes injury or begs for mercy, so that you will stop the attack and give him the opportunity to recover. You only get one chance to surprise an attacker—once he realizes you have had some unarmed combat training he will be more cautious on his next approach. Be assured that he is a cunning animal of the streets and will not be deterred by your small amount of training—just more cautious.

In conclusion. It takes special training to be able to kick effectively, but more importantly, it takes experience to know exactly when to kick or strike back. This experience can only be gained through a professional CQB program where emphasis is put on realistic scenarios that replicate tactical confrontations. With all this in mind, kicking is still one of the best unarmed methods for "putting the hurt" on a would-be criminal or terrorist. We have long known that pain is a good teacher and extreme pain is an extremely good teacher. Use it to your advantage.

*U.S. Marines practice front kicks*

*Axe kick*

*Basic Aikido wrist lock*

*Wristlock used as a control technique*

# 9.

# JOINT LOCKS & BREAKS

The technique of applying pressure to vulnerable joints has several applications within a CQB program. These range from simple control techniques, to grip breaking, to disarming procedures. The amount of damage that these techniques cause is dictated by the amount of control or pressure applied by the user. Most joint locks begin with control and moderate pain, but can be continued to the point of breaking, when such force is justified.

The STTU joint locks, control techniques and breaks were developed from aikido and judo with some karate thrown in for good measure. All techniques are divided into two categories: **hard options and soft options.** A soft option is a law enforcement control technique where no permanent damage is justified. A hard option is for nasty situations where full force and bone breakage is needed. The choice of soft or hard option is generally made according to the type of assailant and his level of aggression/ threat. All soft options are designed to be converted to a hard option when needed.

**JOINT LOCKS**

Most joint locks center around the wrist or elbow and involve manipulating the joint to the point of considerable pain. The technique needs to be not only painful, but should put the victim in a position of disadvantage where he cannot continue his assault. He should also be positioned to where he cannot move without your assistance, and the hard option (kick, strike or break) is available to you.

We have found that modified aikido wrist locks work well in an HRT environment. They are quick, simple and quite painful. Often times the pain alone will readjust a villain's attitude very quickly. (See photos)

In training, the trainees must show considerable control and maturity when first learning these techniques. They must be shown that any horse play or over enthusiasm can result in breaks and dislocations. Once the movement has been mastered, trainees must apply these locks to the point of pain, and immediate submission by their training partner. If these techniques are not applied to the point of pain, then trainees will never get the correct "feel" for the lock. A submission can be in the form of a tap-out or verbal command. Many instructors with a strong martial arts background us the Japanese word to surrender, "Mate!", pronounced "martay!" .

In situations where you are fighting for control of a weapon, the weapon itself can be used to add leverage to the technique. Beware of the sharpened edge on a knife blade or the muzzle on a firearm. This aspect of joint locks will be expanded in the chapters on disarming and retention.

## BREAKS

Breaks can occur in two ways. Firstly by applying a joint lock past the point of pain and onto dislocation. Secondly, by controlling the limb with one hand and delivering a strike with the other. The wrist is usually the target of the first variety, while it is the elbow that is broken with a hammer fist, elbow strike or direct pressure.

Anytime joint locks are used for the purpose of disarming or controlling an armed assailant, no mercy need be shown and breaking is quite justified. When confronted with a knife, gun or broken bottle there is no margin for error or room for gentle techniques. Control the weapon and break the arm as quickly and efficiently as possible.

Another target of opportunity for locking and breaking techniques is the fingers. Do not hesitate to peel away an uncooperative person's fingers and apply pressure—breaking if justified. This is not difficult under ideal training conditions, but considerably harder when hands are wet or gloved.

## CONTROL TECHNIQUES

Control techniques are joint locks taken to the point of pain, where the assailant is immobilized but not injured. To compound the effectiveness of control techniques we recommend that the victim be slammed into a wall, vehicle or onto the floor. A solid structural barrier will restrict the suspects avenues of escape or movement; give you added leverage; and add effectiveness to the technique.

Attempts to control determined criminals or terrorists is discouraged unless the controller has sufficient armed back-up. By closing on a cunning suspect prematurely, one risks being disarmed or over-powered. DO NOT UNDERESTIMATE YOUR ENEMY.

To take control of emotionally or mentally disturbed suspects, who may be unarmed but still a threat, it is recommended that two or more operators team up for the assault. If a weapon is involved, one team member can control the weapon hand, while the other goes for the choke or knock-out.

In all cases, suspects should be cuffed, taped or tied as soon as possible. This is most easily achieved when one operator controls the hands, while the other applies the flex-cuffs or tape. Cuff before searching, and search before transporting.

Final note. All joint locks, control techniques and breaks must be done with speed and conviction. If you show any hesitancy, the victim will see it coming and you will have a real fight on your hands.

When dealing with multiple assailants, there is no time for soft options. Hit hard, hit fast and move.

Recognizing that others may be physically stronger than you, be prepared to step back and resort to firepower, before you are immobilized or disarmed. If your weapon has jammed, then try to maneuver the assailant and yourself in to the best position to give your partner to get a clear shot. This is a life or death business. Someone fighting for possession of your weapon is a lethal threat to you, your team and the hostages.

*Modified wrist lock*

*Joint pressure break*

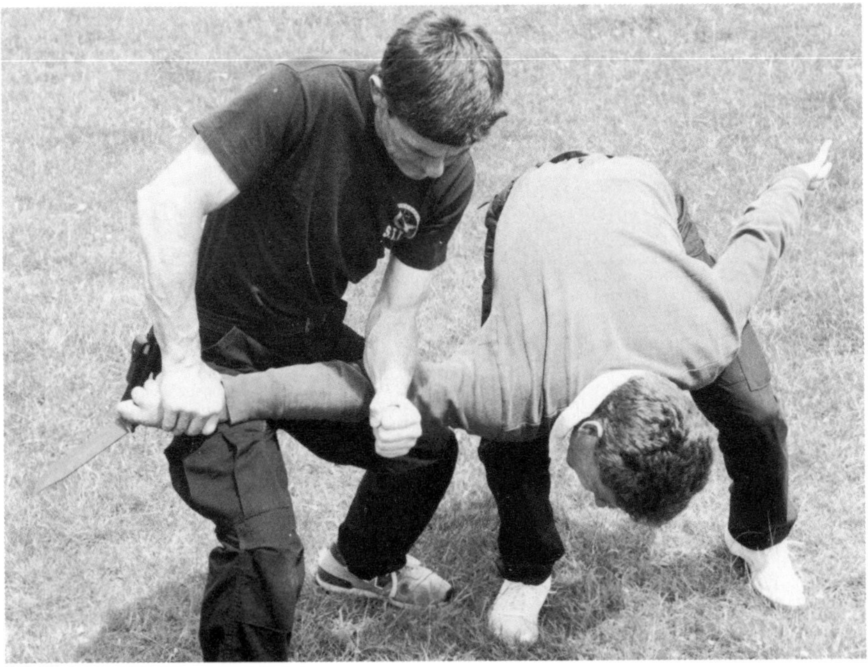

*Strike to break joint*

*Three-man control team*

*Strangle to subdue suspect*

**Hip throw**

# 10.

# THROWS

Hostage rescues and close quarter confrontations are not the time or place to be getting involved in wrestling matches. However there will be times, at the end of a counter attack, when the enemy can be thrown to the ground to avoid escaping the follow up. Throwing techniques can also be applied in situations where an adversary has closed distance and is now too close to strike. Some grappling and throwing techniques are therefore justified within a comprehensive CQB program.

Another useful application for throwing techniques is to drop innocent by-standers, disoriented hostages or emotionally stressed family members that may get in the line of fire or path of the assault. After the deployment of stun grenades, flashbangs, smoke or gas there will be considerable confusion and panic within the barricade location or aircraft.

Practicing throws during training is relatively easy, however performing them in full kit (vests, boots, gas masks, weapons, etc) is a little more challenging. Most of the throws utilized in CQB have their origins in judo, but have been modified so as to be effective in a restricted space. The throws must be short, fast, simple techniques that will drive an opponent into the deck without any unnecessary grappling. Most do not require gripping of the tunic as in the traditional judo form. They are more of a pushing/ controlling/ tripping technique that can be utilized in conjunction with strikes or joint locks. There is considerable emphasis on control of the head—for where the head will go the body must follow.

In addition, several of the aikido joint/wrist locks can also be used to throw or project an individual. These are based more on pain compliance, balance and momentum.

The key to all throws is breaking of the individuals balance by pulling or pushing his upper body outside of his power circle. An individual has a certain range of motion and balance before he becomes unbalanced. A throw is simply a matter of making that person exceed that range and then checking their attempted movement with a part of your body to effect the throw. A little strength and body weight will always serve well to help them on the way.

A throw by itself is seldom incapacitating unless the person can be thrown into a concrete wall or off of a high building. The trainee must be taught to immediately follow-up the throw with a series of strikes and kicks or a gun shot.

Throws used to get hostages out of the line of fire, if they are disoriented or deafened by the stun grenades, are identical except without the follow up blows. Upon entry all shooters should be yelling "Get down—stay down" to the hostages, but often times this will go unheard or unheeded. Physical persuasion will be required to clear the aisles and corridors. Once a person is down, a boot placed on their back or head may be sufficient to control them until the shooting stops.

There are primarily five types of throw to consider:

1/ The hip, shoulder or leg throw, effected by gripping the assailants arm, body, tunic or web gear.
2/ The knock down, effected by sweeping the enemy's legs out from under him or by stamping at the knee area.
3/ The wrist-out throw, which is the result of an aikido wrist lock taken to the point of pain compliance and body-weight projection.
4/ The arm crank throw, achieved by combining the assailants momentum with pressure to the elbow and shoulder.
5/ The face throw, achieved by grabbing the assailant's face and head, pulling it violently to the rear, and then throwing directly downward.

## BREAK-FALLS

To avoid unnecessary injury and build confidence, all throw training should be preceded by the practice of break-falls. Break-falls are widely used in judo and aikido, to protect the participants while still permitting completion of the throw.

There are two methods of break-falling. One requires slapping of the arm and hand against the ground to arrest momentum; the other involves rolling to dissipate energy. The most important aspect of both methods is that the chin be kept tucked into the chest to protect the head.

Where possible, throws should be practiced on padded gym mats. If these are not available, a grass or soft sandy area would be an alternative. Surfaces that are too soft, or sand that is too deep, will only serve to hinder the movement of the feet needed for clean throwing.

**One-arm shoulder throw**

**Rear reaping throw**

**Groin throw**

*(continued next page)*

*Face throw*

*Basic choke hold being used to subdue an armed assailant*

# 11.

# CHOKES & STRANGLES

Over the years, both the police and the military have made use of chokes and strangles. The controversial police choke hold was used to subdue emotionally disturbed individuals and PCP users, by rendering them unconscious. The military has always had a use for strangles, either to eliminate sentries quietly or to snatch prisoners from behind enemy lines for interrogation.

Provided the victim does not have a weak heart or breathing disorder, he can be rendered unconscious with no permanent visible injury. Chokes and strangles play a big part of sport judo competitions and training, and occurrences of individuals getting strangled unconscious are not uncommon.

Before going further we need to differentiate between chokes and strangles, since physiologically they are quite different. A choke occurs when pressure is applied to the throat, more specifically the wind-pipe, to a point where the victim cannot breathe and the lungs are unable to function. When this occurs, carbon dioxide builds up in the system and the body (brain) is starved of oxygen. If the choke is held on long enough (30—90 seconds) the victim will be rendered unconscious—and if pressure is continued, will eventually result in death.

The effectiveness of a choke may depend on whether the victim just inhaled or exhaled; physical condition/neck muscle development; level of exertion to fight the choke; determination; and size. It will also be influenced by how firmly the user can apply pressure to the throat; the exact placement of that pressure; and how well he can control the victim's response.

A strangle on the other hand, is created when blood flow is interrupted to the brain. This requires pressure to be applied to the sides of the neck, the carotid arteries and the jugular veins. The carotid artery carries oxygenated blood to the brain. When external pressure is applied, blood flow is interrupted, the brain is starved of oxygen and unconsciousness arrives very quickly. Continued pressure will result in permanent brain damage and ultimately death. Pressure to the neck can also trick the body into supplying less blood to the brain than is really needed (carotid sinus reflex).

Being choked (starved of air) is a slow, uncomfortable experience compared to a correctly applied strangle. A choke targets the front of the throat while a strangle is applied to the frontal sides of the neck. The lungs can go far longer without air than the brain can go without a regulated blood flow and oxygen, making strangles not only painless, but faster. The danger is that strangles have a more immediate and significant effect on the brain as opposed to chokes which are really only a form of induced suffocation.

Our experience in competition judo has shown us how to easily recognize the difference between chokes and strangles. With chokes, there is usually some gagging sounds, considerable struggle, a contorted face and finally unconsciousness, if there is no submission. The harder one struggles, the fast one will pass out. Strangles on the other hand are usually quickly applied and within seconds, the victim goes limp and is rendered unconscious. When the strangle is released the victims will regain consciousness within several seconds, with no memory of how or why they blacked out.

Chokes and strangles, like all CQB techniques, must be applied quickly and with conviction. If not, the victim will have time to resist, tense his neck muscles, pull his chin in and affect an escape. At best you may end up with a head-lock that does not render the person unconscious.

**Basic strangle**

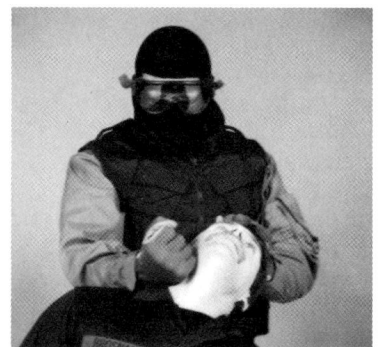

Since it takes two hands to perform an effective strangle or choke, it is essential that the operator have armed back-up, to at least control the victim's weapon and limit the thrashing around. Sentry elimination and prisoner snatches are ideally done with a three man team. One to strangle and silence the sentry; one to take control of his weapon; and one to supply cover with a suppressed weapon.

*Web strike to the throat followed by an iron-claw grip on the windpipe*

**WARNING**

All CQB training should be carefully supervised—especially when working with joint locks, breaking techniques, chokes and strangle. Strangles must be released as soon as the person goes limp or is rendered unconscious. In training, participants should be applying chokes and strangles only to the point of discomfort and submission—not unconsciousness. At the first signs of choking, pressure build-up or dizziness, the victim must be taught to tap out. Verbal submission will be impossible because of the pressure on the throat. If a person is rendered unconscious by accident, they usually will revive themselves within 10 to 30 seconds. If they do not the instructor and trainees must be ready to perform rescue breathing or CPR immediately.

*It is important to break the victim's balance backwards when strangling.*

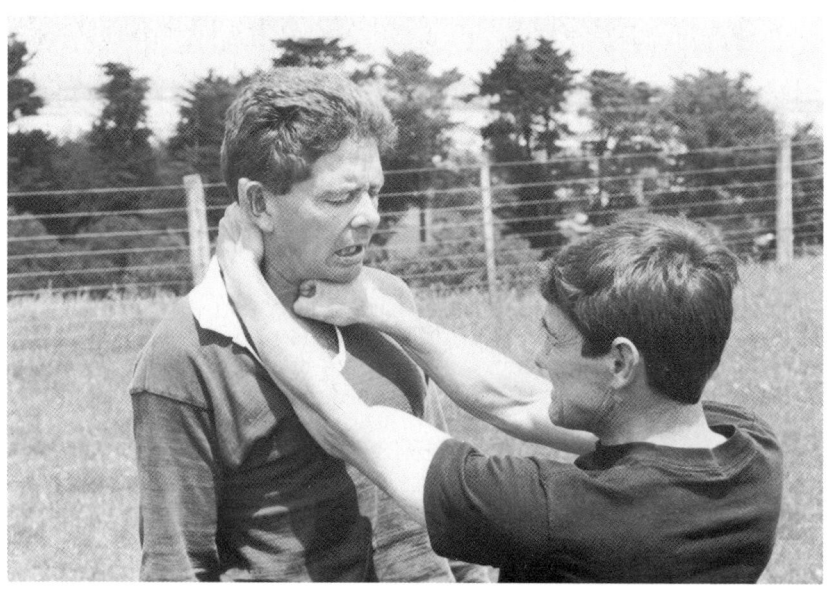

*Punches to the throat can double as chokes.*

*Hammer punch to the side of the head*

*Note control of the weapon.*

# 12.

# DEFENSE AGAINST IMPACT WEAPONS

When placed in the position of having to deal with a stressful confrontation that could result in injury to ourselves, it is part of our primal survival instincts to grab any available object and lash out with it. Criminals and crazies that find themselves cornered without more sophisticated weaponry(a gun), will also try to improvise with some tool or hard object.

The defense against these improvised weapons can be divided into two categories: **blunt impact weapons** or **sharpened edged weapons**. Both groups can be sub-categorized dependent on whether they are short or long weapons. Knives and edged weapons are covered in the next chapter so for now, we will concentrate on blunt impact weapons.

## SHORT WEAPONS

Weapons that fall into the short range category would be clubs, unbroken bottles, saps, sandbags, bricks, vases, hammers, and short lengths of iron bar or pipe.

Short impact weapons are considerably less dangerous than edged weapons unless one is struck from behind. If one can see the attack coming it does not require a tremendous amount of training to turn the situation to one's advantage.

There are three predictable factors involved in the use of short impact weapons:
1. The attacker must close distance to launch the attack.
2. Short impact weapons are usually unidirectional. That is they are swung in one direction as opposed to jabbed or slashed.

3. The head is usually the target of all attacks. The intention being to render the victims unconscious or bludgeon them to death.

Knowing these facts, it is not difficult to anticipate when and how the attack will be launched, and how best to counter it. In most cases the counter attack will involve body shifting to avoid the arc of the weapon, a good strong block and then a series of counter punches and kicks. In blocking the club or bottle, one should avoid meeting the impact square on with the forearm. Rather deflecting the blow with an angled block (see photos).

There is considerably less importance placed on controlling the weapon itself during counter attacks against impact weapons. Unlike a knife or gun that must be controlled at all times, clubs lose all their potential for damage when motion has been arrested.

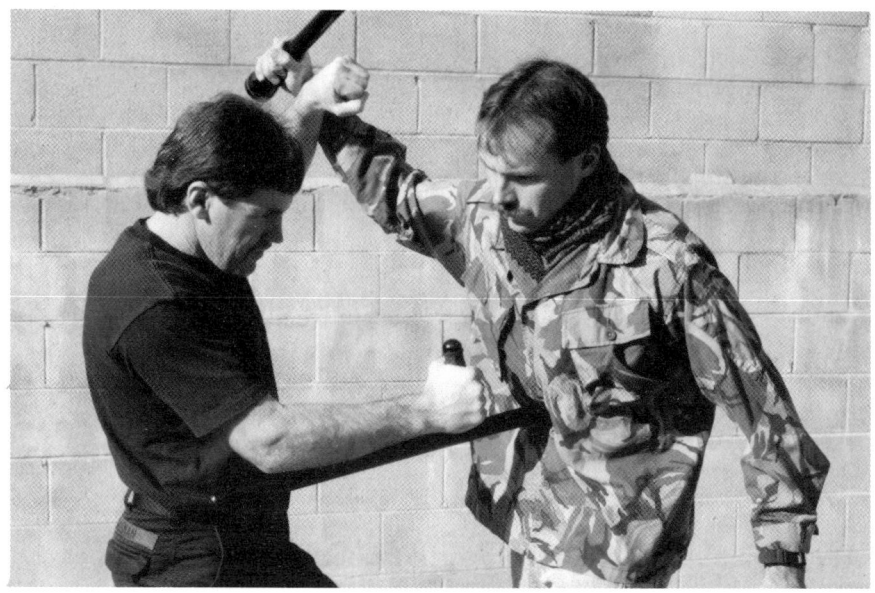

*Note the angled rising block.*

In training, time should be spent trying to read the attacker and analyzing his movements. Is he angry or enraged? Is he on balance? Does he look fast and agile? How is he holding the club? When will he initiate the assault? Will the swing come from the top or from the sides? Am I free to shift, block and counter?

## LONG WEAPONS

Impact weapons that fall into the long category would be baseball bats, broom handles, staffs, lengths of iron bar or pipe (over 3 feet), wooden swords, chains and car antennas. The difference here is that the attacker does not have to close in; the weapons can be jabbed or swung; and the target could be the head, body or legs.

The most dangerous part of a bat or long stick is the very tip, for that is where the most energy is generated. Avoid the tip by body shifting if it is jabbed or shuffling in or out if it is swung.

The key to dealing with these attacks is in "reading" your opponent. Does he have room to swing? How fast can he swing? Is he pressured for time? Will he act precipitously? Does the staff have a sharpened point? How is he holding it?

The way a person holds a long weapon will give some indication of how they intend to use it and how much experience they have with it. If both hands are together at one end of the staff or bat, this is an indication that the assailant intends to swing it. If the hands are spaced wider, then they may intend to jab or bunt.

The key to the counter attack is to your move. You must **get inside the arc of the weapon**, block or check further movement, and then launch a dynamic series of strikes and kicks. Once the weapon is grasped, you will have considerable leverage that can be used against your opponent. Do not get into a wrestling match over the staff—simply control it and lash out with your feet and knees.

***The block***

***The counter strike***

*Slash-cut to neck*

*Downward thrust*

# 13.
# EDGED WEAPONS

An edged weapon is any weapon that is sharpened and can be used to cut, slash or stab. The knife is the first edged weapon that comes to mind but we must also include broken bottles, swords, bayonets, razors and improvised shivs. The inmates of our fine prison system have become quite creative in the art of sharpening any available object, wood, metal or plastic, into a dangerous close quarter weapon.

Nothing is quite as frightening as the prospect of confronting a determined knife wielding attacker, unless of course we are armed with a superior weapon (ie.a gun). The thought of getting cut, slashed and stabbed, or of seeing our own blood and viscera spilled on the floor, is enough to make any man weak at the knees. It must be understood from the out-set that a knife makes a normally inferior opponent a very real danger, even to a skilled fighter. A small man with a knife has a distinct psychological and physical advantage over a larger, stronger man.

So if all military and law enforcement personnel carry guns, why are we even addressing unarmed knife techniques at all? It is not inconceivable that a patrol officer could be confronted by a knife wielding gang member before he has time to draw his weapon. Or that a SWAT team member's weapon jams or fails to fire in the face of an attack. Normally the partner or back-up man should be able to neutralize the attacker, but things do not always happen as they should. So we train for the worst case scenario—unarmed and no back-up. A position many undercover agents find themselves in.

Although most patrol officers and federal agents wear body armor, and all hostage rescue teams should have raid vests, not all ballistic material will stop sharp instruments. A sharp knife will go straight through the conventional Kevlar soft body armor issued by most agencies. Only the heavier raid vests with ceramic, steel or titanium plates will defeat a knife. Unfortunately these vests still leave the arms, throat, legs and groin exposed. All of which can be cut with frightening and traumatic consequences.

We have found that the best way to eliminate some of the fear involved with knife defenses is to first teach knife handling. Knife fighting has been neglected by the military since the Indian Wars. So unless one grew up in an ethnic environment where knives were a cultural heritage (possibly Sicilian or Latino), there is probably little understanding of the dynamics involved.

Some military special forces units may have a legitimate need for knife handling skills, but for the most part, we teach knife fighting and knife attacks solely for the purpose of developing familiarity and confidence with edged weapons.

## KNIFE ATTACKS

Knife attack training is divided into five areas:

- Selection and maintenance of the knife
- Handling and drawing
- Slashing and cutting
- Punching and thrusting
- Blocking and parrying

The knife, just like the handgun, must be positioned so that it can be drawn and used in one fluid motion. To do this it can be carried on either the strongside or in a cross-draw position. The motion of the draw should be continued into the initial slash cut, and will generally involve closing simultaneously on the intended target.

Many of the same principles used in formal karate can be applied to knife fighting. The importance of speed, power, balance and agility are even more important in an arena where every move can result in potentially fatal wounds.

When using a knife to block or parry one usually punch-cuts directly into the wrist or forearm of the attacker, hoping to sever the muscle or tendons that control his grip. Once the wrists or forearms have been cut, the attacker is considerably less of a threat.

Slashing techniques are intended to create an opening, slow an opponent or better prepare the victim for the final thrust. Slashes cause nasty cuts, severe bleeding and may even sever tendons, but they seldom kill quickly unless the slash is delivered to the throat. The advantage of slashes, when done correctly, is that they require little commitment to the move, no loss of balance and are very fast.

Thrusts on the other hand are killing techniques that require power and commitment. If the thrust is too slow or inaccurate, then the technique will be blocked or deflected with potentially lethal results. Constant practice is required to develop the correct line and steady pressing movement necessary for deep penetration of the blade. This can only be achieved by working against a thick target of some form.

Knife attacks are generally a combination of slashes, blocks, punches and thrusts, as will be seen in the accompanying photographs.

Some of our basic exercises are:

From a strong side draw, thumb to butt—
- Draw, vertical punch cut to the face, downward stab to throat
- Draw, vertical slash to chest and face, downward stab to throat
- Draw, direct thrust to rear

From a cross draw, thumb to hilt —
- Draw, punch cut to throat
- Draw, punch cut to face, thrust to throat Draw, diagonal slash to chest, return slash to throat
- Draw, direct thrust to throat, chest or abdomen
- Draw, punch cut to any exposed limb as a block

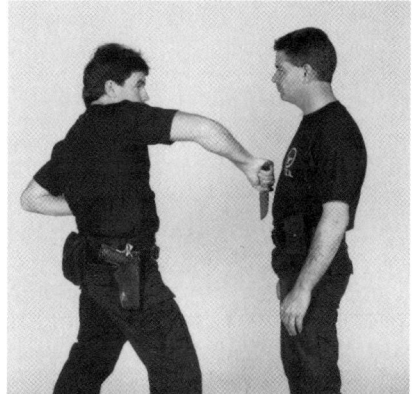
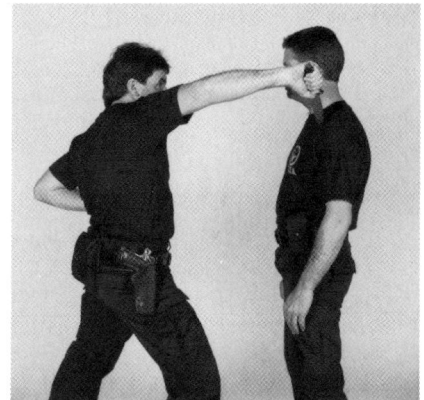
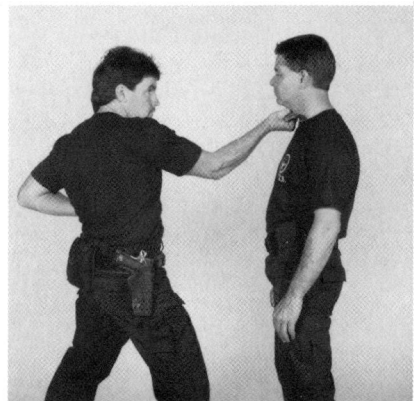

*Cross draw rising across chest and return slash to the throat*

To practice thrusting, one needs to work against a training target that allows for deep penetration of the blade. Unless the thrust is well directed and on line, it is easily deflected. Only by penetrating layers of cardboard or similar material will the trainee get the feel for effective thrusting.

To practice actual knife fighting we recommend the use of rubber knives (Al Mar) with chalked edges. Any contact with the opponent will leave a tell-tale chalk mark on the uniform or body. Rubber is preferable to wood, since even wooden knives can cause injuries.

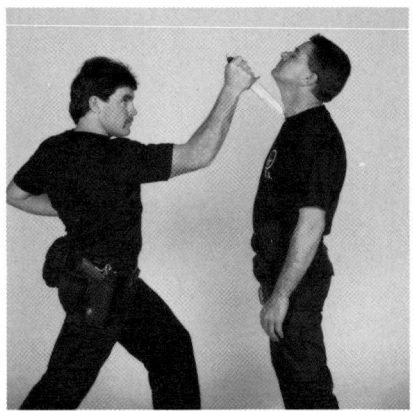

***Strongside draw and vertical punch followed by a downward thrust to the throat***

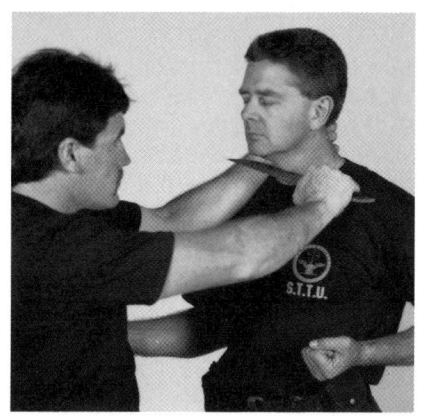
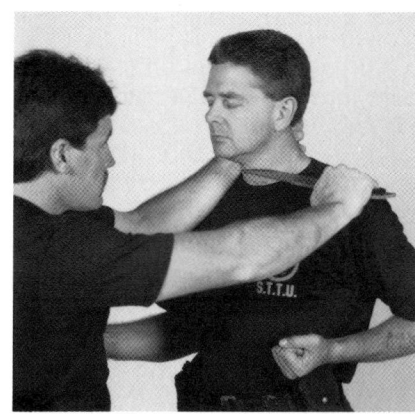

*Knife attacks and thrusts*

## KNIFE SELECTION

Through the ages, the knife has been one of man's most valuable tools, but not all knives are suitable for fighting. Even in the field of fighting knives, there are several styles for specialist tasks. For example, there are knives that are intended to be both survival and fighting knives; others are purely killing/stabbing knives only suitable for thrusting; others are heavy slashing knives only intended for chopping and not suitable for stabbing.

Most commercial fighting knives are either too heavy to move fast, poorly designed or made from inferior materials. They are generally manufactured by people with no concept of knife fighting and are only trying to sell their inferior products by labeling them "Fighting Knives— as used by some Special Forces unit".

A true fighting knife should be a "mission specific" tool. But since we have so little use for pure fighting knives, we tend to carry knives that can do several jobs. The only people who have a use for serious killing knives are special operations personnel tasked with sentry elimination or assassination. But since technology has brought us such a wide array of excellent suppressed weapons, even these people will opt for a more sanitary method of killing.

Some of the best basic designs for fighting knives came out of the First World War (WWI), where the close and dirty aspects of trench warfare made them an essential survival/killing tool. These same designs have been modified over the years, as different metals and technologies become available, but they all have the same fundamental design characteristics.

The best fighting knives are manufactured by a handful of custom knife makers in the United States, such as: Randall, Al Mar, Larry Albach, Col Rex Applegate, Bagwell, etc. There are a few factories such as Cold Steel, Buck and Gerber that turn out a very high quality product, but few compare to a custom made, mission specific fighter.

The more important design features of a fighting knife are:

- Strong and rugged overall design but not too heavy
- Sharp, narrow blade of adequate length to penetrate the vital organs (6"—7.5")
- Light enough to move fast but not so light that it is weak
- A comfortable, non-slip, ambidextrous handle
- Some form of cross guard to prevent the hand slipping onto the blade during a thrust
- A skull crushing butt on the handle
- A secure sheath that still allows for a quick, silent draw

The fighting knife should be able to handle abuse, but not the same amount that would be expected of a survival or camp knife. Fighters are generally slimmer, lighter, sharper and often double sided.

*Killing/fighting knives*

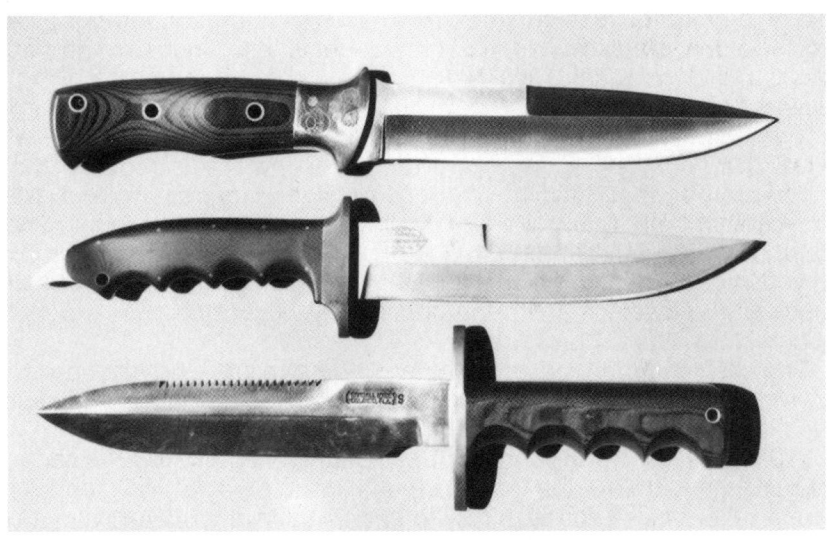

*Survival/fighting knives*

## KNIFE DEFENSE

As stated earlier, regardless of relative size or physical power, a weapon makes even the smallest man a formidable adversary. Immaterial of the attackers experience and training, or lack there of, he will still have a psychological advantage. We all fear getting cut and each of us will react differently to being stabbed or slashed. A shallow slash, although it may produce a considerable amount of blood, will generally not cause the sudden shock and weakness that can accompany a stab wound. Fear on the other hand may paralyze one man but drive another to great feats of bravery or strength. It is therefore important that one **expect to get cut** when involved in the disarming of an armed assailant. In this way the actual injury will not come as such a surprise or trigger a negative shock reaction.

That said, it must also be understood that the brain is still man's most effective weapon (especially when combined with expert instruction and hard training). Your speed, reflexes and training will hopefully make you the victor in a confrontation with someone who is probably not a skilled knife fighter, but merely some scumbag that grabbed the knife as the last act of a desperate man.

A knife adds a lethal capability and extended reach that the user would not normally have with his bare hands. Since it is the knife that is the greatest source of danger, then it is the knife that must get our greatest attention. Even if you are not armed with a conventional weapon, look for anything that may help even the odds against the knife. You may be able to use a helmet, chair or trash-can as a shield; consider wrapping a shirt or jacket around your forearm as some protection; sand, salt or sugar could be thrown in the attackers eyes; or many common objects could be used as a weapon, ie. antennas, ash trays, bottles, statuettes, lamps, fireside tools, etc. There are no rules! This is primal man at his worst.

Now evaluate the situation quickly. How is the knife being held—right or left handed? Is the attacker in a rage or acting in a more cool, calculating manner? If acting out of anger or fear he is more likely to commit to one fast, lunging attack. If he is less aggressive and more threatening, then try to read how he intends to attack and what part of your body is he targeting. With a more calculating knife fighter, is time on your side? Will your partner arrive in time to neutralize the threat with superior firepower? If given the opening, will the felon chose to show discretion and flee the scene?

The cool, experienced knife fighter who plays with you and seeks an opening in your defenses, is a far greater threat than the enraged attacker who will try to rush in and finish you quickly.

Taking all this into consideration, and baring the interference of Samuel Colt, there are three primary principles to knife defense: Evade—Control—Neutralize. Try to remain calm, on balance and alert. Watch the knife, expect the attack and then move quickly and decisively.

1. Evade the initial thrust or attack
2. Gain control of the knife hand
3. Neutralize the attack by breaking the wrist or arm

Knife defenses must be SIMPLE AND EFFECTIVE so as to be easily learned and developed into reflex actions. Knife attacks are generally met by blocking or redirecting the knife arm and simultaneously trapping

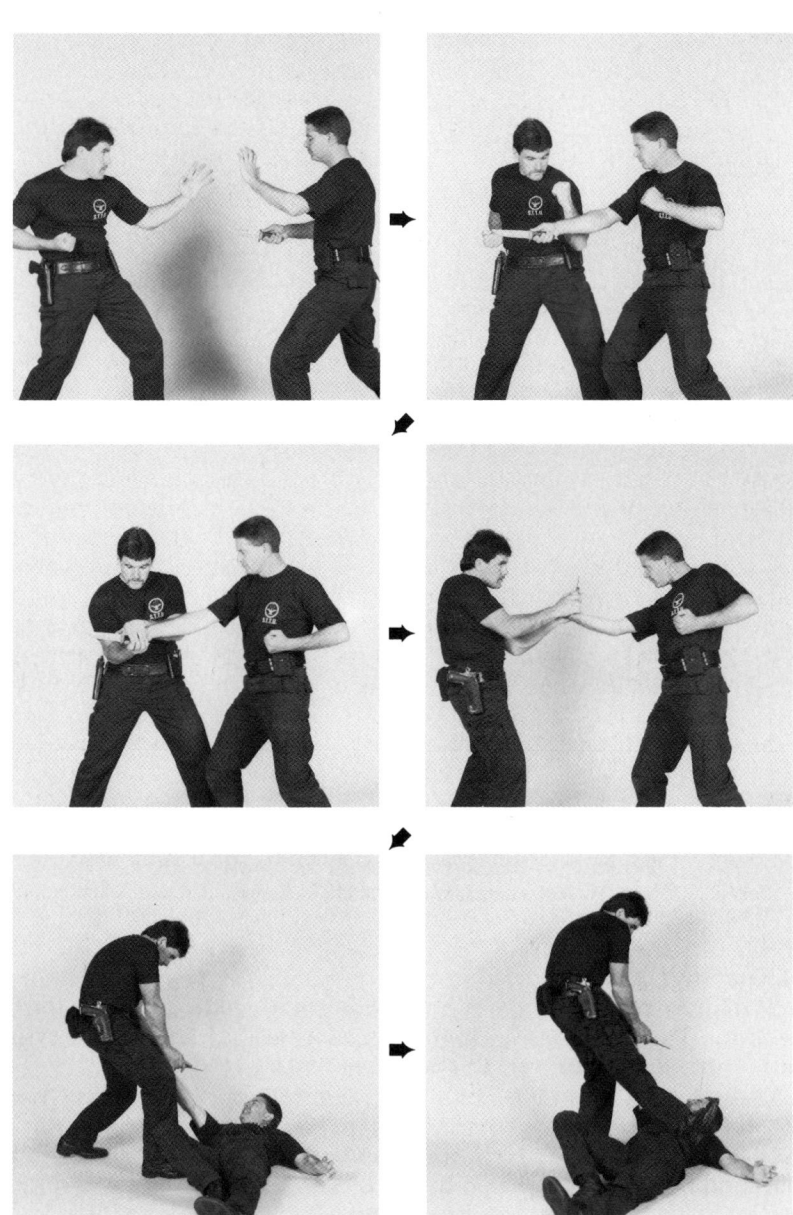

*Knife defense*

*Downward block and web strike/throat grab.
Note control of the knife hand.*

the knife hand. It is important to pivot, body shift or side-step out of the line of the attack, on the off chance that the block may miss its mark.

Ignore cuts to your arms and body, you will survive these. **Think mean.** The prime concern is to stay alive. Once the initial thrust or slash has been diverted and the knife hand controlled, continue the movement into some form of wrist lock or elbow breaking blow. The key objective is to maintain control of the weapon to prevent a counter thrust, and still render the limb useless. There should be no hesitation about breaking the arm since the attacker would have done far worse to you had his knife attack been successful.

The alternative to breaking the arm is to control the knife hand and ATTACK THE ATTACKER. Direct the counter attack towards the most vulnerable and crippling parts of the body. Strike or kick repeatedly until you feel the aggressor buckling under your attack. His use of the knife more than justifies your use of aggressive counter-force.

At this point, police will want to control and restrain the suspect, while military personnel may chose to deliver follow-up blows with the boots or even turn the knife on the attacker. When confronted with multiple attackers one will need break and move very quickly. On SWAT/HRT type operations you should clear the deck quickly to allow the shooters to move to the front.

1

2

3

4

5

6

*Block and two strike combination*

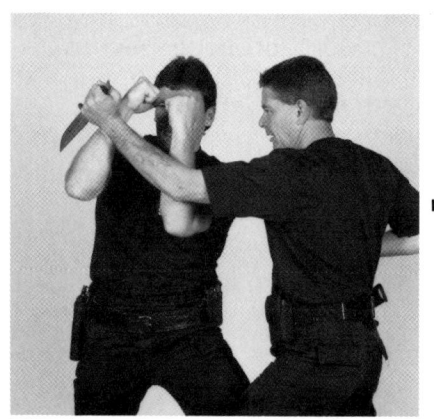 

*Knife parry*

## WARNING
All of the following techniques shown in this chapter should be practiced with rubber knives. First starting slowly to get a feel for the moves, and then gradually building speed and confidence. Eventually trainees should work with sheathed real knives and then finally, when the instructor is satisfied with their performance, bare blades. It is with bare blades that there comes a very real chance of injury. Knife wounds can be both serious and permanent. Bare blades must be used under very controlled circumstances and preferably with the instructional staff playing the role of the knife attackers. In this way they will have more control over the path of the blade and reduce the chance of injury.

FINAL NOTE: No matter how proficient the **unarmed combat expert** becomes at disarming techniques, he will always be vulnerable to even the **smallest weapons expert.**

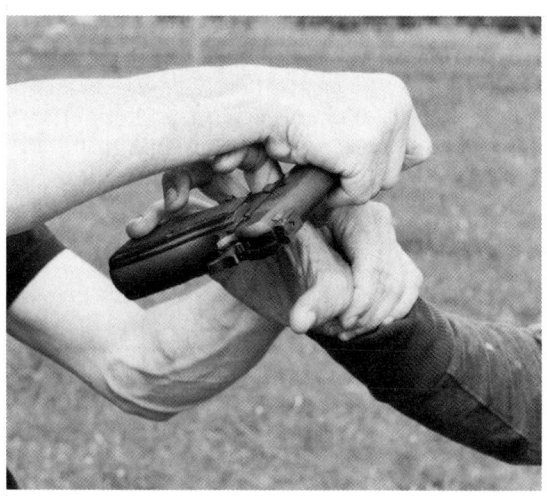

# 14.

# GUN DEFENSES

As with knife defense techniques, the probability of having to disarm a gun toting villain with your bare hands, especially in a hostage rescue role, would be very rare indeed. Any occupants of the stronghold, seen to be pointing weapons at the entry team or hostages, would be immediately neutralized with several well placed shots from an MP-5 or handgun.

The operators in most need of this type of training are patrol officers responding to domestic disputes or public disturbances; embassy staff and security personnel; and undercover agents working without the benefit of armed back-up. All place themselves in positions that could result in their lives being threatened at very close range.

Weapons retention will be addressed in Chapter 19, so for now we will assume that the villain already has "the drop on you"—to quote the cowboys of the silver screen. The reader must understand at this point, that it can be very unhealthy to make a rash or precipitous move against someone pointing a loaded weapon at you. Gun take-aways should only be attempted when:

1/ No other option is available
2/ There is only a single gunman
3/ The gunman is close enough to reach quickly
4/ There is a good chance of success
5/ You are confident in your ability and training
6/ It is evident that the gunman will kill you or a hostage
7/ There is nothing to lose

Gun defenses can be divided into two categories—**Short** handguns such as semi-automatics, revolvers and some small submachine guns; and **long** guns such as hunting rifles, assault rifles and shotguns.

# HANDGUN DEFENSES

Like all CQB techniques, gun take-aways consist of SIMPLE AND EFFECTIVE moves that are quick to learn, easy to perform and capable of becoming a reflex action. This eliminates many of the fancy techniques seen on television cop shows.

As with the knife defenses, the operator must ultimately end up in control of the weapon with a defeated assailant at his feet. We are however, jumping a little ahead of ourselves here.

The first part of any armed confrontation is to evaluate your opponent, if time permits, and consider your options. What is his mental state and will he depart without harming anyone if given the opportunity? Does he seem hell bent on killing someone or is he just threatening out of frustration and fear? How many gunmen are there and what is their spacing or distance? Does he seem to be familiar or competent with the handgun?

In considering your own situation you must decide if you are capable of overpowering this individual? Will your actions endanger others? Do you have room to maneuver? Are there improvised weapons at hand? Is time on your side—is there back-up coming—will the assailant succumb to fatigue?

Try and look again at the gunman's weapon. How is he holding it? Does it indicate training? What type of weapon is it—revolver, double action auto, single action auto, single shot or SMG? Is the weapon cocked? Is the safety on? Is the weapon in battery? Can you see a

*Marine MPs practice handgun disarming techniques.*

magazine in the weapon or rounds in the cylinder? Is the weapon in a state of good repair? All of these points may have some bearing on your chances of success.

Once you realize that life is at risk and you have made the decision to disarm the gunman, there are a couple of prerequisites that need to be in place. Firstly, the gunman must be threateningly **close** to you and you must know **exactly where** the gun is in relation to your body. Keep in mind that the gunman may be behind you and the gun out of sight. It will be necessary for you to wait until the gun is actually touching your head or back before counter attacking.

It is a proven fact that a gunman can be disarmed before he can pull the trigger, provided the distance is short and the move is quick. When you initiate the disarming technique, the gunman must first recognize the move and then make a decision to fire. You will have a slight reflex advantage being the initiator but it is only .2 –.5 of a second.

So the basic principles of gun defense are:

1/ Use speed and surprise to your advantage
2/ Distract the gunman if possible
3/ When you move, move quickly and decisively
4/ Vacate the initial line of fire
5/ Take control of the weapon or gun hand
6/ Break the limb or counter strike with conviction
7/ Continue the assault until the gunman is incapacitated
8/ Maintain control of the weapon

Putting all this together—pivot or body shift and simultaneously deflect the gun hand. The weapon may discharge at this point but the shot will miss you. Immediately take control of the weapon and gun hand, twist and break the wrist, break the elbow or lash out with your feet. Keeping control of the weapon and its muzzle direction, continue your assault vigorously until the gunman is crippled, unconscious or dead. You should now have possession of the weapon.

Some techniques will allow you to disarm the gunman very quickly and shoot him with his own weapon, but do not count on the weapon being loaded or even functioning. Some terrorists and criminals have been shot or arrested in possession of toy guns and inoperable weapons.

Again, if you should feel the gun discharge, you may be deafened, temporarily blinded by hot gases or even creased by a bullet. Ignore these injuries and continue your attack vigorously. The wounds will heal but you have only one life—fight for it.

Understanding how a particular weapon functions may help in your gun take-away. If you note that the safety is still engaged, the weapon should not fire when the gunman mashes down on the trigger. If the weapon is cocked (hammer back), you may be able to get your thumb or finger under the hammer and prevent the weapon from firing. With revolvers, if they are not cocked, grasping the cylinder firmly will prevent it from rotating and the gun from being fired. Some semi-automatics will not function when the magazine is removed, while others can be deactivated by pushing the slide back out of battery.

However, none of these things can be counted on and many similar weapons function quite differently. Others may have been modified after they left the factory. The only thing that can be counted on is to body shift out of the line of fire and get control of the weapon/gun hand. Anticipate the weapon discharging so you will not be surprised when it does. Use that shock action to your advantage.

Handgun take-aways should be practiced from all realistic positions. These include:
  Gun in the face
  Gun to the heart
  Gun in the stomach
  Gun to the side of the head
  Gun to the back of the head
  Gun to the upper back
  Gun to the lower back

After practicing from a standing position, try some of these from a sitting hostage position. Remember, when you can't see the gun, try to feel its exact location with your body—discreetly.

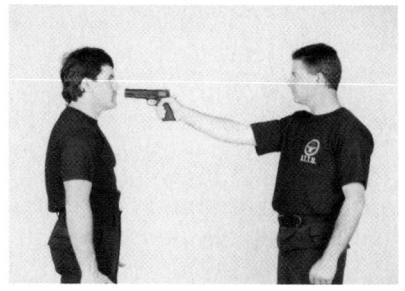

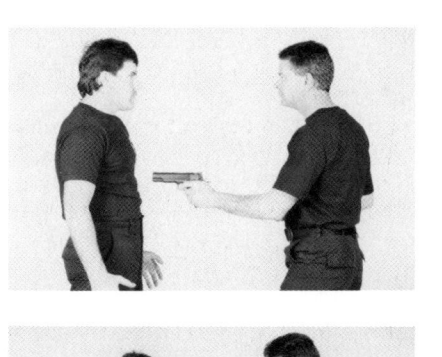

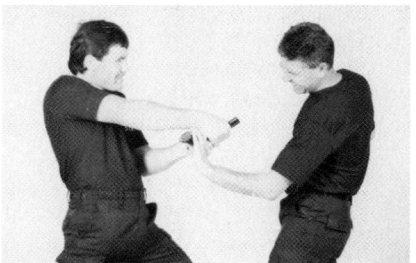
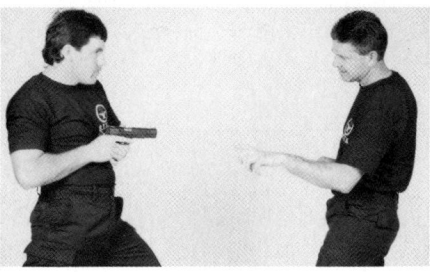

---

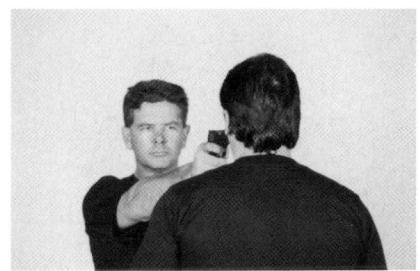
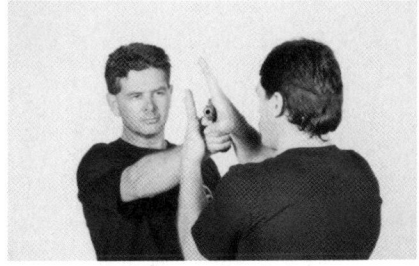

*Move head and control muzzle simultaneously.*

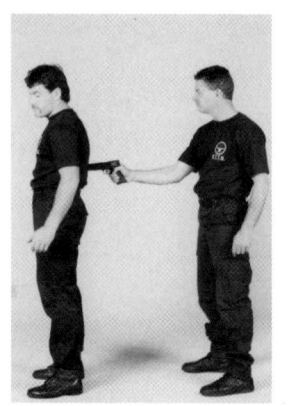  

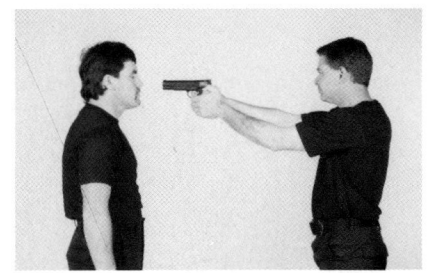

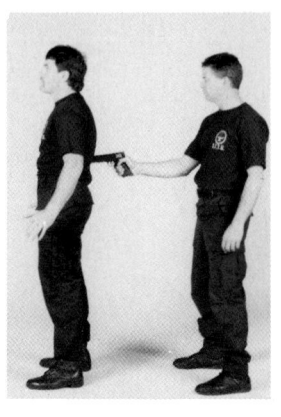  

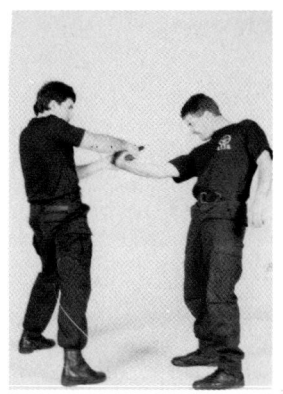 

## LONG GUNS

The key differences between hand gun take-aways and long gun defenses is that you may have added leverage when you grasp the barrel but the gunman is further away from you. So although you may be able to control the muzzle, it may be more difficult to inflict pain or injury on the trigger man. Additionally, the soft body armor that may defeat a pistol bullet will be next to useless against most high powered rifle rounds. Only heavy entry vests with the necessary ballistic inserts will protect against these weapons, and even then there are no guarantees.

The prerequisites are the same as for handguns. Consider the gunman's mental state, his apparent level of training, familiarity with the weapon and willingness to use it. Consider your own options, risk to others and proximity to the weapon. Study the weapon so as to better understand its type, function and capability.

Bolt action rifles need to be manipulated after each shot; assault rifles may be semi-automatic or full automatic—look at the selector switch. Submachine guns may fire single shot, burst or full automatic—they may also fire from an open bolt (Sten, Stirling, Mac, Grease Gun, Uzi) or closed bolt (MP-5, HK53, AUG, CAR15). Shotguns may be single shot, double barreled, semi-auto or pump action. Any weapon that has been fired several times will have a barrel that may be too hot to grasp. Then again, getting burned is preferable to getting shot.

So taking it by the numbers, the sequence of movements is similar to that of the handgun drills. They are:
1/ Know the location of and distance to the weapon
2/ Body shift or pivot out of the line of fire
3/ Simultaneously grasp the barrel and fore-end of the weapon
4/ Expect the weapon to discharge—it will be considerably louder than a handgun
5/ Control the muzzle and try to twist the weapon from the gunman's grasp
6/ Move inside of the muzzle and launch a series of kicks and strikes against the gunman's vulnerable areas
7/ Continue the counter attack until you have possession of the weapon and incapacitated the gunman

**A note of caution.** Avoid pulling the weapon directly away from the gunman as this may cause the weapon to fire, especially if his finger is around the trigger. It is preferable to push the weapon inwards and the muzzle upwards. In this manner the weapon may discharge safely into the air, and the upper receiver or barrel can be slammed into the gunman's face. In addition, fully automatic weapons will tend to climb as they fire.

## FINAL WARNING

Think long and hard before attempting to take a loaded weapon away from a threatening gunman—**you will only get one chance.** If possibility becomes reality—then hopefully your training and reflexes will help send one more terrorist or criminal to meet his maker.

# PART III

# NON-LETHAL OPTIONS

*S.T.T.U. Explosive Entry Class*

# 15.
# ASSAULT CONSIDERATIONS

Close Quarter Battle (CQB) consists of far more than basic unarmed combat, a few knife drills and gun take-aways. It encompasses all the skills required for an operator to survive a confrontation at relatively close range. In a special operations hostage rescue role this is also known as Room Combat. It does not include intelligence gathering, deployment, sniper options or conventional military operations in urban terrain (MOUT). In addition to unarmed combat, CQB does include close quarter surgical shooting, dynamic method of entry, small team drills and hostage management. All of which come under the heading of Room Combat.

When entering a terrorist stronghold or barricade location there are several tactics that can greatly reduce the danger to the team and the hostages. When an explosive method of entry (MOE) is employed, and/or stun munitions are thrown ahead of the team, then in all probability, the occupants will be sufficiently disoriented so as to pose little threat to the assault team.

This level of confusion on the part of the suspects can also be created through the use of diversions, distractions and simultaneous entry through multiple points in the stronghold. Without getting too involved in the complex subject of tactics, which is beyond the scope of this book, it is safe to address the basic principles of room combat—

SPEED
SURPRISE
SHOCK ACTION

When all three of these are utilized by a well trained, well lead, well equipped team, then the probability of success is very high. The entry, room domination, arrest and/or rescue may be achieved without gunfire or loss of life. So if the object of CQB training is to survive a potentially dangerous close quarter confrontation, then the objective has been reached.

## EXPLOSIVE ENTRY

The use of explosive charges, to breach doors or walls into buildings and aircraft, has long been a standard operating procedure for international counter terrorist teams. But unfortunately, because of a lack of training, understanding or expertise, explosive entry has not become common within the law enforcement community. Another reason may be the apparent liability exposure incurred if the charge is excessive.

The two prime advantages of explosive MOE are the almost **guaranteed entry** and the **stun effect** on the occupants. Gunmen and hostages should be stunned to a certain degree, making both parties easier to dominate and control. However, it is not recommended that the breaching charge be placed on doors or walls leading into the "keep"—the actual room where the hostages are being held.

Explosive MOE has been perfected to such a degree that the secondary fragmentation from the door, and the risk of over-pressure injuries to the hostages have been all but eliminated. This should in no way make light of the potential for disaster when working with explosive compounds and initiators in a tactical environment. Explosives are very much the realm of the experienced bomb technician, EOD personnel or specially trained operators.

*Author (right) displays the effect of cutting charges to breach a wall into the stronghold.*

Breaching charges come in several forms from factory made linear-shaped cutting charges to improvised systems made from Det-Cord (primer cord that detonates at in excess of 22,000 feet per second). Another is a caulk-type compound that can be applied directly to a door or pre-made form with a caulking gun. All are usually command detonated with an electrical firing system and blasting cap. Some teams are working with a non-electric firing system called NONEL, but electrically fired systems, even if less desirable, are still the most common.

During explosive MOE training, the team must be protected with Nomex hoods and uniforms, boots, goggles and ear muffs, entry vests and gloves. Trained and experienced explosives handlers must be present, and no one should be involved in explosive entry without formal training and a careful work-up.

If the door must be breached by more conventional non-explosive methods, e.g. battering ram, boot or crow bar, then stun grenades should be dropped through broken windows to temporarily disorient the occupants. Always target **two or more entry points** for breaching in case one is too heavily barricaded to allow entry.

## STUN MUNITIONS

Stun grenades, also known as flash-bangs (FBG), are designed to temporarily stun the occupants of a room, bus or aircraft, so as to give the assault group time to make entry and dominate the stronghold. The stun grenade may well have saved more lives than any other single piece of equipment in the SWAT inventory. Unlike explosive entry, the use of stun munitions has become a standard procedure for most police and federal agencies. On a domestic level, they are being used in raids on gang houses, crack/rock cocaine houses, and for a wide variety of felony warrant services and routine barricade situations. The only place they may not be employed is against drug production labs where there is a high probability of fire or explosion, owing to the presence of volatile chemicals.

Unlike conventional military fragmentation grenades, the stun grenade does not break-up into a storm of small lethal fragments. The body of the grenade is usually made of cardboard, and in some cases, even the fuse mechanism separates before final detonation.

Some of the newer devices are constructed with a non-fragmenting aluminum body that merely vents the force of the charge out of each end and then can be reloaded with a new fuse/charge module. Most stun munitions have a fuse delay of approximately one second so that the grenade cannot be picked-up by the barricade suspects and thrown back.

There is considerable variance in the effect of many of these devices. Some emit a loud bang; some a blinding flash; others both flash and bang; and some are loaded with several submunitions that go off over a few seconds. All in all, the bangs and flashes are secondary to the intended effect of the grenade—to stun. It is the shock wave caused by the rapidly expanding gases that accompanies the detonation that actually stuns the rooms occupants.

Be aware that some commercially available munitions are advertised as "Stun Grenades" while others are "Distraction Devices". The distraction devices came out of a need for a lower powered grenade that would reduce the chance of injuries, and the accompanying liability suits. After all, we do live in a litigious society and who better to sue than a SWAT team, a police department and the city.

Unfortunately, even though distraction devices produce a loud noise and some flash, they generally do not have the power to physically stun a determined gunman. To get the full stun effect there must be sufficient force in the explosion (compound in the grenade) to raise the pressure in the room and physically incapacitate the occupants. The application of one or the other may be dictated by the level of determination of the armed suspects, type of weaponry displayed, age and condition of the hostages and size of the structure. Domestic barricade situations may be solved with a distraction device while dedicated terrorists or drug dealers may be worthy of the full effect of a stun munition.

*Nuclear protection team deploys stun munitions during a training exercise.*

*Graphic display of the effect of two stun grenades*

*Helmets, battering rams and body bunkers have become standard equipment for many agencies.*

## THE ASSAULT

Breaching, either by explosive or conventional MOE, is only the start of room combat. The team must now enter quickly, aggressively and efficiently. The same principles of SPEED, SURPRISE and SHOCK ACTION apply. The assault team must be into the stronghold, covering their assigned AOs (areas of operation), neutralizing the threats and dominating the survivors before the effects of the entry and stun munitions have worn off.

This speed and efficiency, which contributes considerably to safety, can only be achieved through hard training and constant practice. Only when every man understands his role, and the contingencies, will the group begin to function as an effective team. As with the unarmed combat moves, the secret to success is repetition—repetition—repetition, with a constructive critique after each drill. The weapons handling will be addressed in Part 4 of this text.

The important parts of the assault are:
- Know your area of operation (AO)
- Understand your task
- Know your entry point (EP)
- Know your alternate EP
- Know your method of entry (MOE)
- Have an alternate MOE
- Observe safe weapons handling
- Positively identify your targets

It is fine to perfect individual skills, but ultimately, training sessions should end in full team scenarios that incorporate all tactical capabilities. This includes explosive MOE and the deployment of stun munitions.

## SAFETY

All personnel involved in explosive MOE or with stun munitions must receive formal training and be equipped with protective clothing. This includes goggles, vests, gloves, hoods, hearing protection, uniforms and boots.

For additional material on tactics and explosive entry, obtain a copy of ADVANCED WEAPONS TRAINING for Hostage Rescue Teams, published by STTU. Also refer to Appendix A in this text, for additional recommended reading.

# 16.

# NON-LETHAL OPTIONS

AUTHOR'S NOTE: There is really no such thing as a non-lethal weapon. Any tool or weapon when directed against a vital part of the body with sufficient force can prove fatal. A blow of seemingly moderate force, struck in the heat of battle, could result in internal bleeding, permanent brain damage, respiratory arrest or heart failure. In addition, there is no accounting for the medical or physical condition of your adversary. A more accurate but perhaps confusing term would be "low-lethality options". It is the initial intent of the operator that should dictate the correct terminology. If the initial intent is to incapacitate and not kill, even if the adversary dies, the assault team member should not be held culpable.

## INTRODUCTION

There are several alternatives to firearms when it comes to neutralizing a specific threat. In some instances, the use of deadly force may not be justified, but resorting to bare hands could prove foolish. The police have long had to work within this middle ground, where they are under constant criticism for unnecessary use of deadly force, and heavily restrained by departmental policy and public opinion.

To fill this void there has always been a wide variety of impact weapons and specialty low lethality munitions available. These impact weapons range from short range weapons like the common baton, to longer range weapons such as rubber bullet guns. The specialty munitions range from hand-held aerosol sprays to launchable gas generators and stingball grenades. When used at close range, these all become part of the CQB program. They are tactical options.

It is only in the United States that military forces cannot be deployed for civil problems. As a result, there are many international military counter terrorist teams that require non-lethal police options for use in civil insurrections, riots and against unarmed criminals, gangs and insurgents. Some teams have even gone so far as to develop their own mission specific impact weapons and methodology.

When deploying with impact weapons, it is important to understand that situations can change very quickly and escalate into deadly encounters. For this reason, anytime operators are deployed with impact weapons as their primary weapon, they must be buddied-up with a cover man armed with a firearm and ready to shoot. The alternative, when entering an open air riot situation, is that the assault team can be covered by elevated snipers and supported by an armed rescue squad.

Riot control, open air options and long range weapons are beyond the scope of CQB and room combat, so this text will only touch on these weapons briefly. The close quarter weapons will be addressed in more detail.

## BATONS

Civilian law enforcement and military police have historically found a need for a wide variety of hand held impact weapons. Just as the criminal element has utilized clubs, bats, bars and chains to express their anti-social tendencies. The police tools range from the small leather sap, through the short truncheon supplied to Commonwealth police and navy shore patrols, on up to the longer night sticks and side-handle batons favored in the United States.

It would seem that the length of the baton is directly related to the level of threat found in any given location. An example of this can be found in New Zealand where the regular police carry a short concealed baton, while the special task forces carry the PR-24, or what they call the "long baton". Japanese riot police, when confronted with an ugly crowd, will utilize batons all the way up to samurai sword length. For CQB we must first understand the need and application of this tool, before we can establish an optimum size and design.

When it comes time to commit a special operations assault team, it is usually already recognized that the situation is beyond conventional methods. Therefore the threat level is significant, even if the suspects are not armed with firearms. Violent criminal elements, gang members or mentally disturbed individuals, are all capable of inflicting serious injury by use of improvised weapons. They do not need to be treated gently and will often require considerable physical force to be subdued.

The reasons for not entering with drawn weapons, more often outside of the United States, could be one of the following:

—The suspects are on drugs and incapable of recognizing the threat or of reacting logically

—The barricade suspects are mentally or emotionally unstable and may attack without any sense of personal danger or consequence

—Gang members may find it necessary to fight back rather than lose face in front of their peers

—Public opinion or departmental policy may not allow for the use of firearms against "unarmed" civilians

Valid or not, there is still a place for an impact weapon. If the team is comprised of patrol officers, then they should already be familiar with either the straight stick or the side handle baton (PR-24). It may be best to give advanced training in the CQB applications of this weapon rather than trying to introduce a new system. Military teams and dedicated counter terrorist teams can seek out a weapon that is most suited to their role.

The baton, or combat staff as it is referred to by some teams, should be short enough to carry easily and swing in a confined space, but long enough to have sufficient weight and reach to be effective. Somewhere in the range of 28" to 36" will work, with 30"-31" being optimum. The staff should be constructed of sturdy materials and be comfortable to grip. This type of staff is very versatile and can be used to block, chop, bunt, prod, break, control and strangle. Room combat does not usually allow enough space for a good baseball type swing, so training emphasis must be placed on short chopping and prodding techniques.

*Note: Blows to the head can be lethal.*

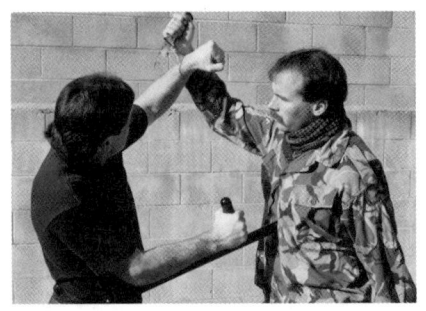

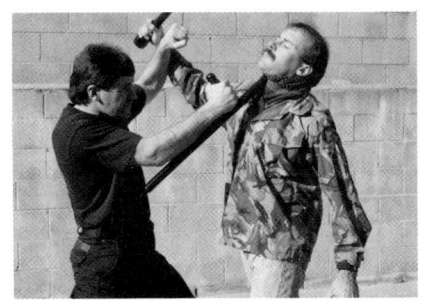

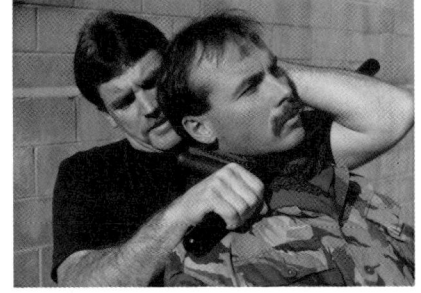

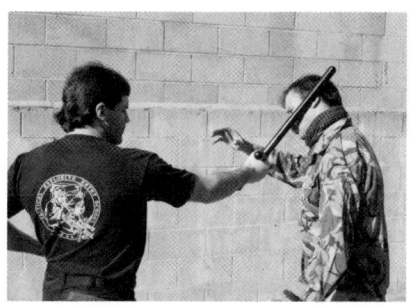

## IMPACT PROJECTILES

Weapons that fire "non-lethal" impact rounds are usually reserved for use in outbreaks of civil disorder, prison riots and against large unarmed lunatics or PCP users. These weapons are usually multi-purpose guns that can fire gas, smoke, buckshot or illumination rounds. They range in caliber from 12 gauge to 40mm with the 37mm guns being the most common.

The **12 gauge** projectiles come in three forms: a single rubber rocket; 3 large rubber balls; or 9 buckshot sized rubber pellets. All have the potential of being lethal at close range and are generally only harassing projectiles at longer ranges.

The **37mm** can shoot a single large rubber bullet, a bean-bag type projectile, and in some cases a wooden slug. One popular weapon with correctional facilities is the ARWN 37mm with a revolving magazine arrangement.

An additional option is the use of stingball grenades to soften up a crowd. These are hand thrown devices, usually airburst above a crowd or in a room, that emit a hail of rubber balls. These units were used with considerable effect to end one riot in the LA County Jail. Mattresses being held up as barricades had defeated the use of the 37mm projectile guns, but an airburst stingball cleared the cell block very quickly.

*ARWN 37mm*

*Stingball grenade*

## GAS

Since the inception of the stun grenade, the use of gas by hostage rescue teams has become all but non-existant. Tear gas, whether CS or CN, can be a double edged weapon creating more problems for an assault team than it is worth. It does cause discomfort and confusion for the suspects, but it does not incapacitate a determined gunman.

On the other side, it requires that the entry team wear gas masks and hoods, hindering communications and reducing visibility. Gas may also create panic and confusion amongst the hostages; restricting breathing; making them believe the structure is on fire; and send them rushing for the doors.

However, since gas does have an application in prison riots and against barricade suspects that are not holding hostages, we will look at the variety available.

Gas grenades can be hand thrown or launched from a shotgun or gas gun. They have both pyrotechnic and non-pyrotechnic methods of delivery and dispersal. Be aware that pyrotechnic delivery systems will cause fires if they come in contact with flammable materials, ie. carpet, drapes, furniture, etc.

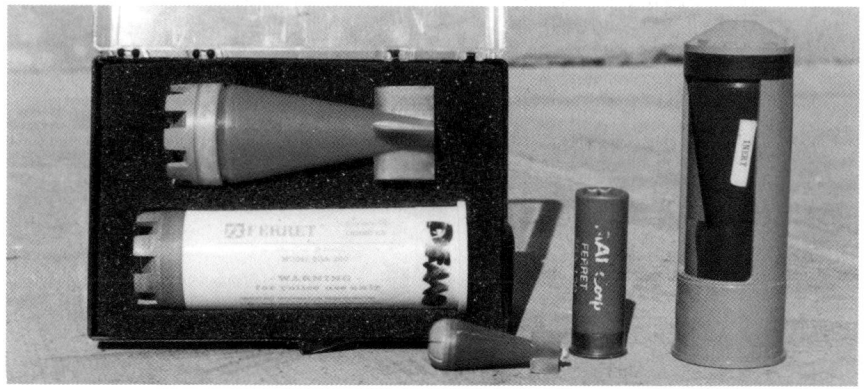

*12-gauge and 37mm Ferret rounds*

One launchable, non-burning delivery system that is popular is the Ferret round, which is available in 12 gauge, 37mm and 40mm. The Ferret is a fin-stabilized projectile, filled with a liquid CS or CN compound, that is quite accurate and will penetrate barricades.

Another option is the hand-held aerosol delivery systems that range in size from the small mace canisters, up through the fire extinguisher type Clear Out and Cap-Stun units, all the way to the large pressurized ISPRA Protectojets. All have a place in the police and military arsenal, but their applications for crisis entry and hostage rescue are few.

## CONCLUSION

Although there are a wide variety of non-lethal options available to a CT, HRT or warrant service team, the threat level will usually justify the use of firearms. Even though there may be some situations where the powers-that-be have requested the use of a non-lethal option, **think long and hard about making an entry with only a stick in your hand.** It is not the politicians, administrators or even Joe Q. Citizen who must breach the door and confront the unknown. When in doubt, take a gun, issue a verbal command, and then prepare to defend yourself. This puts the outcome back into the perpetrator's hands.

*U.S. Marines train in a gas environment prior to overseas deployment.*

# PART IV

# CLOSE QUARTER SHOOTING

# 17.

# INTRODUCTION TO COMBAT SHOOTING

## HISTORICAL PERSPECTIVE

**Author's Note:** Over the last ten years my training philosophies, personal style of shooting, and in more recent years teaching methods, have all gone through several changes—and I hope, are still open to improvement. I do not claim to be the "expert" that has all the answers, but merely a very serious student of shooting who recognizes his own deficiencies, and knows where to look for the solutions to others' problems.

My career in shooting had humble beginnings, some twenty-six years ago with my first air rifle. That was followed by progressively more powerful rifles, a lot of hunting, and some experience in high-powered sporting rifle competitions. It was in my mid-teens that a local gunsmith, small-bore champion and good friend encouraged me to take my shooting seriously, with the words of wisdom—"Accuracy is the product of uniformity".

That piece of advice served me well through-out my rifle shooting career, military service, and right up to the publication of my first book, SNIPER COUNTER SNIPER. It also had application to my first tentative attempts at handgun shooting and field archery.

My thinking started to change in the army with exposure to close quarter point shooting, and later in practical pistol shooting, where time limits were short and adrenalin ran high. Suddenly, the principles of relaxation, breathing control, careful sight alignment and slow trigger squeeze, gave way to a desperate need to shoot faster. Without formal pistol instruction, I began to fall back on my martial arts background—watch, listen, imitate, persevere.

At first I learned by watching the local shooters, studying my own style, shooting a lot and eventually winning on a club level. By setting higher goals, studying the better U.S. shooters, and continuing to shoot several times a week, my scores and times improved. But I still found, by adhering to the basic principles of shooting, I was shooting too slow.

Then something interesting happened. I was shooting the usual combat courses of fire, but did not consciously remember thinking about sight picture or trigger squeeze. Instead, I was concentrating on the match, programming my brain and letting my body do the work. My times improved dramatically and I began placing in the top ten on a national level.

I was passed thinking about the mechanics of shooting, and was now enjoying the experience of muscle memory, a trained eye and a conditioned body. Combined with increased confidence and a more relaxed competition attitude, brought about by previous exposure to match stress, experience and continued success.

None of this was apparent at the time, since my mind was too occupied with just shooting, moving, reloading and shooting. It was not until I started teaching that I began to seriously analyze my style of shooting, and attempt to verbalize it for my students. My initial successes as an instructor were very encouraging. Students appeared to learn fast, show rapid improvement and draw confidence from their new found ability. Even experienced police officers immediately understood the value of our style of shooting, and improved on all their previous qualification scores.

As a serious student of combat shooting, I continued to study the other top shooters on the circuit, to see if we were all on the same track. Although the styles of shooting, the mechanics, varied to some degree, the attitudes and dedication were very similar. The true winners were the ones who honestly loved to shoot and explore the outer limits of their ability and equipment.

As practical pistol competition moved away from the realities of combat pistolcraft; trick holsters and $3000 compensated guns became the order of the day; I started putting more time into teaching and developing tactical shooting programs. The first realization was that the law enforcement and military communities were several years behind in their concepts of combat shooting, and the in-house instructors were inflexible dinosaurs.

Thanks to the promotion of practical pistol shooting by a few top shooters who had turned instructor, and the willingness of some forward thinking agencies to look outside of their own academies, modern pistolcraft slowly crept into the system. DELTA, SEAL Team 6 and FBI-HRT were the first to send their shooters out for training. Soon, other law enforcement and military groups followed, but it was not until the mid-eighties that our (the modern combat shooters) techniques became the rule instead of the exception. Unfortunately, most agencies do not allow their personnel the time or ammunition to become even proficient, let alone fast and consistent.

To this day, few police or military shooters ever shoot enough to graduate beyond the mechanics of basic shooting and into the realm of truly advanced combat shooting. The ability to transfer conscious thought away from the gun, onto the targets, and shoot by feel, muscle memory and fast visual acuity. Only through concentration, lots of shooting, a positive attitude and the motivation to push one's self beyond the limit, will one become a faster, more natural shooter. This ultimate plane of combat shooting cannot be taught, it can only be experienced, and then only after a lot of time behind the gun. However, we can reduce the training time by laying a solid foundation and directing the shooter's energies into the most productive exercises.

## STATE OF THE NATION

It is hoped that the reader, if presently attached to a special operations team, is already an above average shooter and only looking to apply his skills, that are already well learned, to CQB and room combat. Whether military counter terrorism, DEA raid team, police SWAT or FBI hostage rescue, close quarter shooting comes down to the same objective—TO HIT WHAT YOU SHOOT AT WITH SPEED AND CERTAINTY.

Your survival, the safety of the assault group, that of the hostages and the success of the operation all depend on your personal ability with a weapon. Knowing when to use it, when not to use it, and how to use it when necessary. This is true for every member of the team, from the most experienced assault group commander to the newest replacement. Standards must be set for selection on to the team and for continued service with the team. These standards must be realistic, inflexible and high enough to guarantee the shooting skills of all involved. The only way to develop confidence in your own shooting ability, and that of your fellow team mates, is by knowing that everyone met and exceeded the minimum standard—but not with ease.

Selection and qualification standards should reflect the realistic needs of the team and the environment in which they are expected to operate. Obviously DELTA team can set a far higher standard than that of a small municipal SWAT team. They have a larger number of troops to chose from, are involved in higher speed operations and would be confronted by a more dangerous enemy. In addition, the international political ramifications of a mistake on DELTA's part could be far more damaging to US foreign policy than that of any local warrant service.

However, at the risk of contradicting myself, it is important to realize that even the smallest local police raid carries all the risk of death or injury that would be found in any larger CT operation. In fact, U.S. law enforcement personnel, especially teams such as LA Sheriff's Special Enforcement Bureau or Florida's Metro-Dade SWAT, do more raids, dynamic entries and warrant services, and are involved in more shootings than any international team will ever see. To make truth be known, personnel from SEALs and DELTA train with large county and municipal teams, just to learn from their day to day experience—actually doing what the military can only train for.

International terrorist activity and sub-national conflicts such as Beirut, Grenada, Panama and most recently the Gulf crisis have given the army and navy, through SOCOM, the opportunity to put their training to the test. An important aspect in the development and training of any special operations group. There is only so long that skills, honed to a razor's edge, can be maintained in peacetime. Training must have purpose and direction, but at the same time be flexible and based on a changing reality.

European teams seem to have less problem testing their skills. Especially teams like the British SAS with their on-going conflict with the IRA, not just in Northern Ireland but on an international level. The Falklands campaign also gave them an opportunity to test their more conventional "green role" skills, along with their amphibious counterpart unit the SBS, Royal Marine Commandos.

Now, bringing it all back to the subject at hand—CQB. The reader must realize that the skills required by all teams are very similar. It is only the nature of the enemy and complexity of the operation that may change. Operations always come down to going through doors and shooting accurately—CONSISTENTLY. To do this calls for a certain understanding of fundamental and advanced shooting techniques, and the tools of the trade.

Competency does not require multi-million dollar training facilities, computerized ranges and high-tech shooting houses. Any small SWAT team can get hours of beneficial training out of a ply-wood mock-up of a two room building. In reality, that is all they would be called upon to assault. The more that is expected of a team, the more sophisticated the training structures required. This is why full time teams like FBI-HRT have large training budgets, ample ammunition, and elaborate facilities. The team must train for the expected task and threat level.

Note: Readers may find that we cover the topics of weapons selection, modification, maintenance and basic training rather briefly in the next two chapters. This is only because these subjects have been well covered in our previous texts on hostage rescue and special weapons training.

> "Weapons are an important factor in war, but not the decisive one; it is man and not materials that count."
>
> Mao Tse-tung
> (1893-1976)

# 18.
# THE WEAPONS

Firearms play a significant role in CQB training since most tactical operations are of the high risk variety, against armed suspects. Before studying the principles of close quarter shooting, it is important to have a good working knowledge of what constitutes a suitable combat weapon.

For CQB and room combat we need not concern ourselves with the longer range sniper weapons, high powered assault rifles or squad automatic weapons. Our previous book, ADVANCED WEAPONS TRAINING, covers all these weapons and accessories in some depth. With this in mind, we will move directly into the handguns, submachine guns, and to a lesser degree, shotguns suitable for close quarter fighting.

## HANDGUNS

Although some spec-ops units consider the handgun a secondary weapon, only to be used if the SMG malfunctions, we consider it a very effective primary weapon. Since most HRT teams are drawn from the law enforcement community, and the handgun is the standard sidearm carried at all times, it is therefore logical that this is the weapon one should be most proficient with.

Once a team acquires automatic weapons they tend to neglect their handgun skills. If an operator can shoot a handgun well, he can master any SMG with ease. But if he does not dedicate time to his pistol shooting, he will lose these skills very quickly.

Another reason for emphasis on the handgun is one of budget. A team will shoot less ammunition and attain a higher degree of accuracy with their handguns than they will with the hungrier burst fire weapons. A good handgun is a valuable tool and far more versatile when working in a covert, undercover or plain clothes mode.

A combat handgun must be first and foremost a **reliable** weapon with a proven record of good service under prolonged use. In addition, it should have the following:

- Simple, rugged design with good ergonomics
- Sufficient power and penetration to reliably stop an assailant
- Reasonable accuracy, but not so tight that it is unreliable
- Good clear, rugged sights for rapid alignment
- A clean, crisp trigger
- Adequate magazine capacity for serious combat/multiple targets
- A corrosive resistant, no glare finish

Finally, it must be controllable enough to allow for rapid shot placement on multiple targets. Or, second and third shot follow-up on a single determined attacker (double and triple taps).

Most teams are currently using high capacity nine millimeter (9mm Parabellum) weapons, but several are still holding onto their tried and proven forty-five (.45ACP) Government Models. The future may see some teams going to the new family of ten millimeter (10mm) and forty caliber (40 S&W) handguns. The revolver has been all but discarded as a serious hostage rescue weapon, owing to its meager capacity (6) and difficulty to reload quickly.

Many an argument has been started over the topic of which caliber is the "best" man-stopper—usually by armchair commandos and the "experts" who write for gun magazines. Well let's put it all to rest here and now. Any of the current combat calibers (9mm,.45ACP, .357, 10mm), in the hands of a good shooter, will do the job just fine. It is shot placement that is the single most important factor in stopping capability—not bullet design, velocity, diameter, or construction. As long as the bullet has sufficient power to penetrate the intervening body tissue, to reach a vital organ, everything else is secondary.

All team members should be issued the same type and caliber of weapon. New weapons should be thoroughly tested (500+ rounds) before going into the field or used on operations. The only modifications permitted on the weapons are ones that enhance performance, and do not include non-functional gadgets that could loosen and become a liability. Acceptable modifications could include: changing the grips to better suit the shooter; adding high visibility sights; smoothing the double action trigger and cleaning up a single action one; polishing the feed ramp; opening the ejection port; adding night sight inserts; or anything that will improve reliability. Remember—the affect that weapons' **modifications** have on performance is negligible when compared to serious **practice**.

Feeding problems and malfunctions with handguns can usually be traced to bad magazines or inferior/incompatible ammunition. The easiest way to identify these problems is to try the weapon with proven reliable magazines and high grade ball ammo. Magazines should be marked and numbered to facilitate the identification of one that consistently causes malfunctions. If magazines have been dropped on a hard surface, the lips may have become bent, changing the angle of attack of the round trying to transition to the chamber. Some can be repaired, others will have to be discarded.

*Current U.S. military issue Beretta 92F*

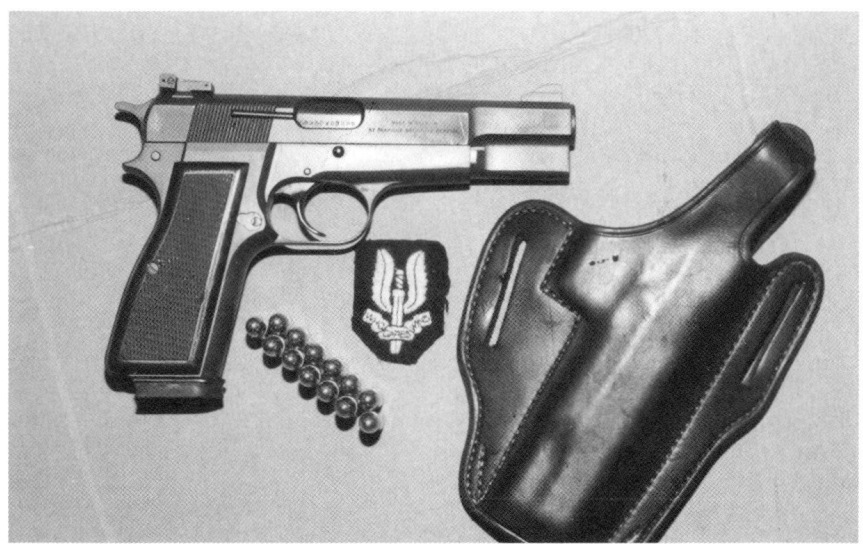

*The Browning High-Power utilized by many elite teams*

*Sure-Fire light mounted SIG 220 and 226*

*H&K P7-M13 utilized by GSG-9*

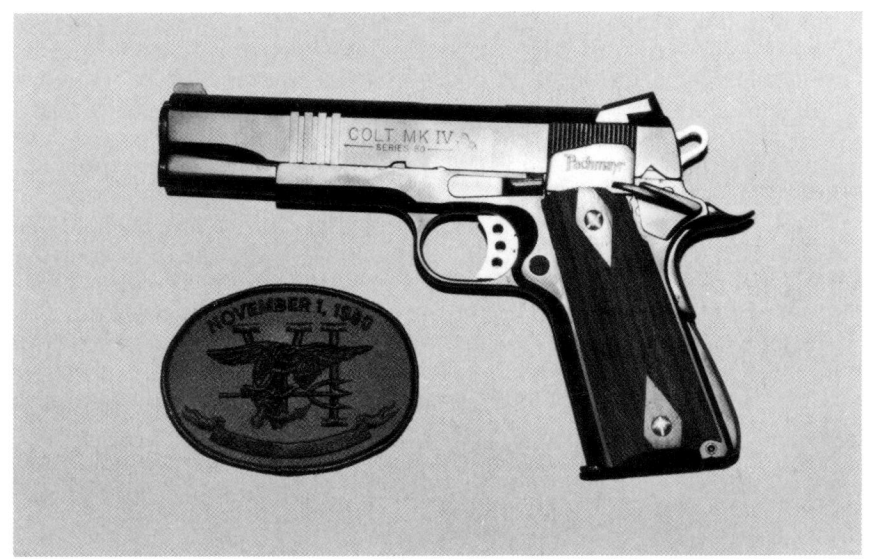

*D&L custom Colt Government Model — available in 9mm and 45 ACP*

## SUBMACHINE GUNS

The primary advantages of the submachine gun are large ammunition capacity, increased fire power and compact size. But more importantly, it is the number of accessories that can be attached to enhance performance for room combat. Lastly, and not insignificantly, it is the confidence gained by the assault team members from the weapon's appearance and increased capacity/ rate of fire.

In selecting an SMG, it must have not only the capability of rapid fire at close range, but also extremely accurate select fire. In close proximity hostage situations, it is important that the assault group can engage the terrorists with precise, confident, surgical shooting, without endangering the hostages. A "hose job" is not an acceptable form of shooting when dealing with raids or rescues.

There is also the psychological effect that the SMGs may have on an adversary. Drug dealers, gang members and even terrorists may be less inclined to try and shoot it out with the authorities, when it is noted that the raid team is armed with automatic weapons. That said, do not count on the mere presence of a SWAT team and superior fire power to terminate a crisis. There are always political or religious fanatics who will gladly give their lives for the cause. Not to mention society's ample distribution of criminals and crazies. If you flaunt it, be prepared to use it.

As with any weapons system, the selection criteria should be: rugged reliability; time proven performance; accuracy; quality construction; and availability of spare parts and service. The selection of a submachine gun may well be the easiest choice your teams has to make. There is one that has become the standard for all police and military special operations, and the one by which all others are judged—the H&K MP-5, and its related system.

The MP-5 has become the trade mark of the world's elite—SAS, GSG-9, GIGN, DELTA and SEALs. On a local level, LASD-SEB, LAPD SWAT, FBI-SWAT and FBI-HRT. This is not to suggest that the MP-5 is the only suitable weapon out there, it is simply the most popular.

While DEA and some SEAL and DELTA operators are making good use of the newer Colt CAR-15s in 9mm and 5.56mm (.223), the Italians still utilize the Beretta M-12S (9mm) and the Israelis the venerable UZI.

Where there is a risk of being caught in the open, or a little more

***U.S. Navy Seal Team diver comes ashore with an MP-5 submachine gun.***

*Seal Team leader with MP-5*

*MP5-SD2*

*MP-5 with light mount*

*Author with MP-5K*

range and power is called for, many teams have also adopted the H&K-53—a 5.56mm version of the MP-5. US Customs teams are working with the Steyr AUG in .223 Win, while others still have the Ruger AC556 in inventory.

In our experience, the MP-5 and the HK-53 make for a very good partnership, since both function the same and require no retraining. If the team is already familiar with, and using the M-16, then the CAR-15s in 9mm and 5.56mm may be a better option.

One of the submachine gun's most significant advantages over the handgun is the number of accessories that can be integrated into the weapon system.

These include but are not limited to:
- Integral fore-end light mount for darkened rooms
- After market flashlight brackets such as the B.E.A.M.
- Conventional scope sights for longer range precision shooting
- Red-dot type laser projectors for enhanced shot placement
- Invisible laser designators to be used in conjunction with night vision goggles
- Suppressors for those times when noise could compromise an approach
- Blank firing attachments (BFA) for training purposes
- Fixed or folding stocks

The most important accessory being the light mount. Most raids take place at night and room combat is usually in poorly lit structures. It is difficult, at the best of times, to juggle both a flashlight and a weapon, let alone open doors and handle the occupants. With the light attached to the weapon, the shooter can conveniently bring the weapon to bear, where ever the light is pointed. Light mounts are not intended as aiming devices, but definitely hasten and simplify the aiming process.

*M16-A2 (M-4) Colt carbine (5.56mm)*

*H&K 53 is very controllable — even on full automatic fire*

*Federal agent trains with Steyr AUG*

*Beretta M-12S*

*MP-5 with laser projector*

## SHOTGUNS

The shotgun is an excellent multi-purpose weapon in many situations, but its role in hostage rescue is restricted. There is no denying the awesome knock-down power of a full load of magnum buckshot at close range, but the shotguns limited magazine capacity (4—8) and marginal accuracy make it unsuitable as a primary entry weapon. In addition, the shotgun's length makes it difficult to get through doorways and the heavy recoil only slows second shot follow-up.

Any assault weapon intended for CQB, must be able to make guaranteed close proximity hostage shots. The increasing spread of the shot pattern (approximately 1" per meter) will only serve to endanger the hostages, fellow team members or other by-standers.

Where the shotgun can be used, is as a perimeter or entry weapon. Perimeter teams can use the shotgun to fire Ferret rounds or launch gas grenades into a structure. Entry teams can use the shotgun with the frangible Shok-Lock rounds to blow hinges or locks, especially on interior doors. Some team members will carry a sawn-off Remington 870 in a leg holster or on a sling, for the sole purpose of blowing locks and hinges, when internal door charges (IDs) are neither available nor appropriate.

If for budgetary or policy reasons the team is stuck with the shotguns as an alternative to SMGs, then the shooters have two options. They either use their handguns as the primary entry weapon, or put a lot of time into understanding shot spread and perfecting scalloping techniques for partially exposed headshots. It is possible but it takes hard work and continuous practice. One of the best shotguns for this type of work is the Benelli Super 90, marketed by H&K in the United States. It is an 8 shot weapon with excellent handling characteristics and accuracy with either buckshot or solid slugs.

*Author demonstrates the application of a shotgun in hostage situations.*

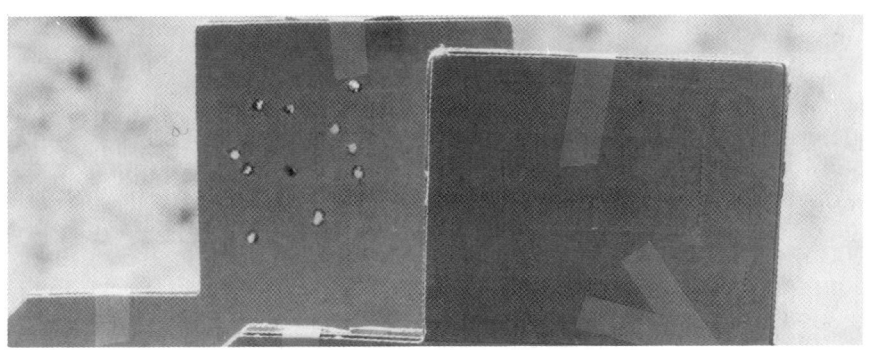
*Shotgun headshot with buckshot*

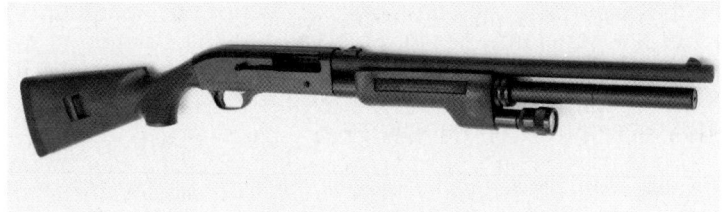
*H&K Benelli Super 90 with light mount*

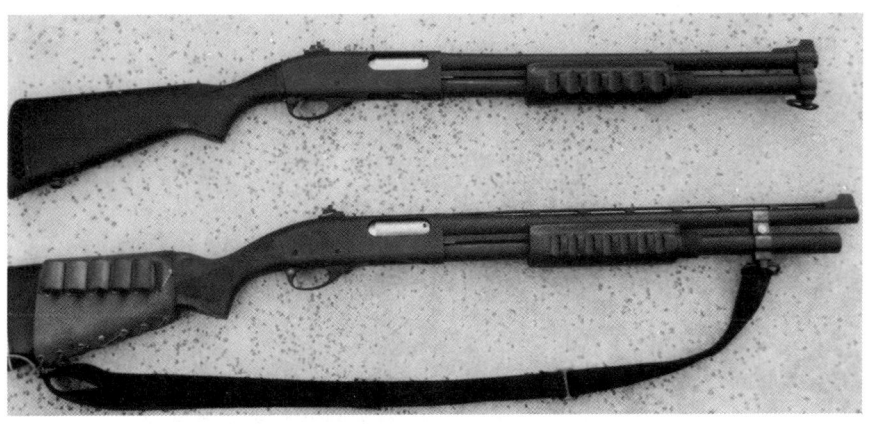
*Custom Robar 870 shotguns*

## AMMUNITION

Ammunition is probably one of the single highest budgetary expenditures incurred in the training of a special weapons team. It is not unusual for high speed teams to shoot 500 to 1000 rounds per week, per man. We often shoot 200 to 300 rounds per day, per man when involved in firearms training. After initial weapons skills have been mastered, a maintenance program should still allow each man 100—200 rounds per week. Agencies operating on less than 100 rounds per month are incurring a tremendous liability exposure.

The basic criteria for all ammunition selection are:
- The ammunition should come from a large, reputable manufacturer
- It should be of a consistently high standard
- It must function reliably in all weapons
- It should have sufficient penetration to reach a vital area
- It should be accurate
- It should be purchased in bulk for consistency and economy

Avoid the expensive trick ammunition, "super hot" loads and "killer" bullets that are constantly being advertised as the solution to all problems. They tend to be too expensive to train with; give erratic feeding and function; and are seldom very accurate. Go for consistency, reliability, accuracy, quality and economy.

*Snipers must be supplied with the highest quality match grade ammunition*

*Colt 9mm SMG, used by DEA, with Sage light mount*

*Note Bolle tactical goggles and Tac-arm lite.*

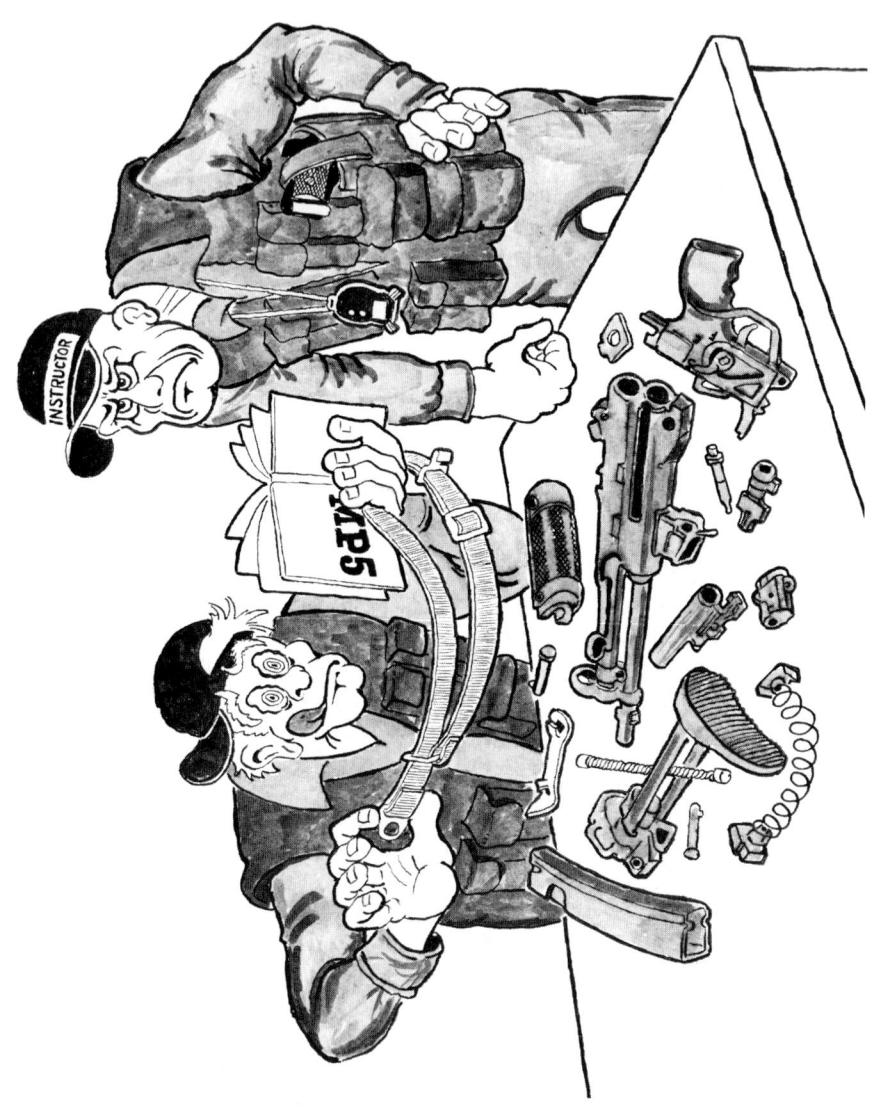

# 19.
# SAFETY AND FUNDAMENTALS

Advanced close quarter shooting conjures up images of masked individuals in nomex suits, running through the killing house, engaging multiple, threatening targets with devastating precision. That may well be the end product, but if one does not have a firm grip on the fundamentals involved, that image will remain an unattainable dream.

Secondly, if the team has not been taught safe weapons handling from the start, there is a high probability that training will be interrupted by injury or death. Anytime shooters begin moving with loaded firearms, there is an increased opportunity for accident. This can be avoided by an increased awareness, strict range control and attention to some basic rules.

## SAFETY

1. Treat all weapons as loaded
2. Control the muzzle at all times
3. Do not handle weapons unnecessarily
4. Keep the finger off the trigger except when shooting
5. Do not point a weapon at anything you do not wish to destroy
6. Never leave a weapon unattended
7. Obey all range commands immediately

In addition, every shooter should act as a range safety officer and be able to stop training anytime he sees a dangerous situation developing. The sign of a good rangemaster is a man who prevents accidents by his awareness of the potential for danger, inherent with each new exercise.

All shooters and range personnel should wear ear and eye protection at all times during live fire training. It is also strongly recommended that body armor be worn on the range and in the shooting houses. If the team must fight in it, they should definitely train in it, not just for protection but to get used to the bulk and weight of the entry vests. Something that is often neglected by teams in warmer climates.

No matter how experienced the group, a safety lecture should precede all training sessions, especially when doing live fire entry exercises or running a hot range (weapons loaded at all times). Another potential for safety violations occurs when shooters are transitioning to a new weapons system, ie. revolvers to DA semi-automatics, or assault rifles to shorter submachine guns. Trainees must be competent and confident with a new weapon before they are pushed to the limits of speed and accuracy. Under stress, unfamiliarity can quickly escalate into an accidental discharge, or worse, a gunshot wound.

## TRAINING PROGRESSION

Adherence to a formal training program based on safety and a building block progression, can greatly reduce the potential for accidents. By gradually building up to a required skill level, based on performance objectives, all participants have the opportunity to work out any problems before they become a safety hazard. A sample progression could be as follows:

Safety lecture
Weapons familiarization
Basic slow fire
Rapid fire; single and multiple targets
Basic fire with movement, use of cover, etc.
Individual entry drills, no live fire
Individual entry with slow fire
Individual entry at increasing speeds
Team entry, walk through with dry fire
Team entry, slowly with live fire
Team entry, medium speed with live fire
Team entry, high speed with dry fire
Team entry, high speed shooting

Training only moves to the next level when the instructor or team leader is satisfied with both safety and shooting standard.

## FUNDAMENTALS OF COMBAT MARKSMANSHIP

No matter how good a combat shooter one aspires to be, one never graduates from basics. A significant percentage of all training time must be devoted to practicing and testing the fundamentals of marksmanship. In addition, the shooter that lacks a solid foundation in slow-fire target shooting, will never become a great high speed combat shooter. Granted, hitting large steel targets at close range will give one the perception of being "hot", but when it comes to realistic room combat, the hits just won't be there. Tactical shooting that requires head shots on close proximity hostage targets, in low light, from less than ideal positions and under the stress of time or physical danger, will cause one's confidence and performance to come apart at the seams.

The two most important fundamentals of accurate aim-fire are sight alignment and trigger control. The ability to concentrate on the sights, hold them on target, and then release the trigger without disturbing the sight picture. If one can do this, then the shots will hit their intended mark. The only difference between a combat shooter and a bull's eye shooter, at this point, is that the combat shooter must do it quicker, with a slightly greater acceptable margin of error.

Combat shooting does not call for the Olympian's ability to hit a small X-ring at long range, but simply the ability to hit the "kill-zone" at reasonable combat distances, consistently. The foundation of this ability still lies in the basic shooting fundamentals of:

**STANCE**—A natural and comfortable shooting position that allows flexibility and freedom of movement. There is no rigidly enforced "correct" stance. Most shooters are currently using a modified Weaver or Isosceles position—which ever works best for them and supplies the necessary balance.

**GRIP**—A firm comfortable grip on the weapon, not so tight that the weapon shakes, but firm enough to control recoil and deliver several accurate shots quickly.

*Aim-fire is the foundation of all combat shooting*

*Shooter on left is very accurate but too slow. Shooter on right has reached a good harmony of speed and accuracy.*

*Most handgun shooting principles can be applied to the SMGs. Aim-fire training is equally important whether on select fire or burst.*

**SIGHT ALIGNMENT**—The ability to focus on the front sight, while looking through the rear sight, and still be conscious of target location. Where a bull's eye shooter aims for a specific point on the target, the combat shooter uses more of an **area aiming** technique.

**TRIGGER CONTROL**—The ability to slowly increase pressure on the trigger, without moving the muzzle laterally or vertically, and achieving the ideal surprise break. This process is quickened and compressed for rapid-fire combat shooting, but the muzzle is still kept within an acceptable range of movement.

**BREATHING**—Under ideal conditions the breathing pattern is used to help slow the heart rate and achieve an almost tensionless condition in the chest. The combat shooter, operating under tight time limits must learn to break the shot at the first acceptable sight picture. The only influence over breathing is the shooter's cardiovascular conditioning.

**FOLLOW THROUGH**—Follow through (or remaining on target) ensures that the shooter does not start moving the muzzle to the next target before the bullet has left the barrel.

**THE DRAW**— The draw is an important part of combat shooting and has a significant effect on the time the shooter takes to break the first shot, and the correct final grip on the weapon. The holster must allow the shooter to draw the weapon with the same grip that he would use for shooting, with total economy of movement. The progression of the draw is:

    Keep your eyes on the target/threat
    Grip the weapon correctly and unsnap the holster
    Clear the holster by keeping the wrist straight, tucking the elbow in and rolling the shoulder
    Take the shortest line from the holster to the target. This is achieved by punching out and elevating the muzzle simultaneously
    The safety is released and the trigger finger inserted into the trigger guard as the muzzle comes on target.

**DOUBLE ACTION TRANSITION**—The ability to go from the heavier first round trigger pull, to the lighter and crisper consecutive shots with the double action semi-automatic pistol. An acceptable degree of accuracy with the first two rounds can only be achieved with diligent practice and a lot of shooting.

**RELOADING**—A competent shooter must be able to reload any issued weapon, handgun, SMG or shotgun, quickly and efficiently. Recognizing that it is a tactical error to shoot a weapon empty, there are still times when the shooter will need to make a quick reload. Either in the face of danger or during a tactical pause; for instance, prior to entering a second or third room.

The reader must keep in mind that the above fundamentals are only a foundation for combat shooting. They should be practiced regularly, but many will be consciously discarded when one begins to explore their personal limits of high speed shooting. With time and practice, many of the mechanics of shooting will become second nature and be performed without conscious thought.

Many police and military agencies still persist in doing all training and qualifications on the 25 yard line, even though we know from experience that confrontations occur at much shorter distances. Continued shooting at longer ranges, with proportionately slower time limits, will only serve to frustrate the shooters and develop poor conditioned response.

FBI statistics for officer involved shootings in the United States, indicate that the bulk of firearms training must be spent on close, fast confrontations, under less than ideal conditions. The same stands true for room combat and SWAT type operations. This is not to say that no shooting should be done at longer ranges, simply that the training time and shooting distances be divided up to reflect reality. These needs will vary from military to law enforcement and criminal to counter terrorist roles.

Where formal team training time is limited, individuals should be required to work on the basic shooting fundamentals on their own time. Instructors, range time and ammunition should be available to the serious shooter who wants to maintain skill levels or remedy deficiencies. Team training time should be devoted to more advanced exercises, individual room combat and team drills.

**Rapid reload**

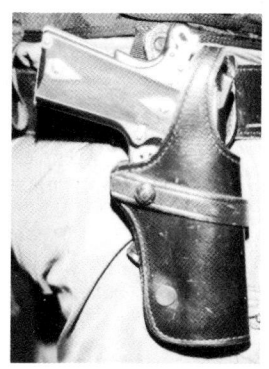 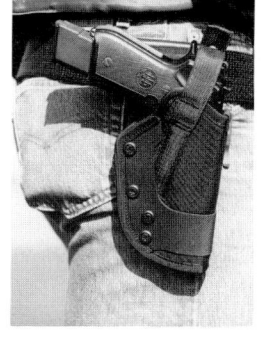 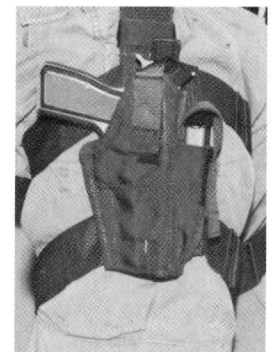

**Davis**  **Uncle Mike**  **Eagle**

**The Draw**

*Marine MP SRT team practice close-quarter aim-fire on paper targets*

*Various steel targets*

*Note shooter back-up in this disarming drill.*

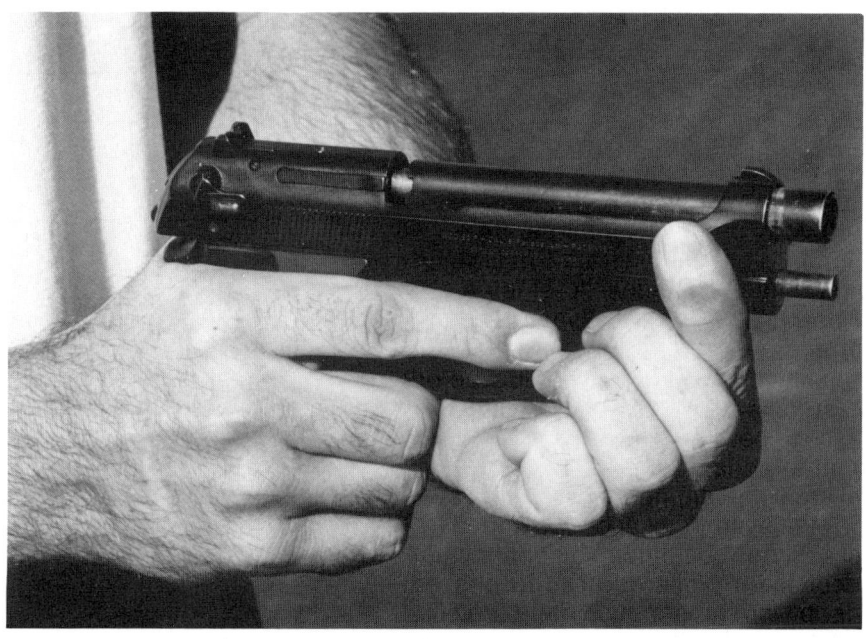
*It is important to do a "press check" to ensure there is a round chambered, prior to going operational.*

# 20.
# CLOSE QUARTER SHOOTING

When it comes to close quarter shooting, we are addressing the needs of the individual under room combat conditions. Once we have mastered individual skills, we will be free to address the increased complexities of team drills.

The conditions found in room combat are:

High stress, high speed shooting
Relatively short ranges; 3 feet to 45 feet.
Poor lighting conditions
Limited space in which to maneuver
Multiple targets/assailants
Hostages in close proximity to armed suspects
Smoke, noise and confusion

Without throwing the trainee in at the deep end, start a CQB shooting program by reviewing his ability to hit a single target, with reasonable speed, at seven to ten yards. Once he has demonstrated this essential skill, depart from conventional aim fire and begin to program his hand, eye and brain to function on a faster, more coordinated level.

For a shooter to improve at this point, he must first recognize the deficiencies in his ability. He must overcome ego and do some serious self evaluation. Perhaps he is fast but has the occasional miss; perhaps he is very accurate but lacks any real speed; perhaps single targets are no problem but multiple targets are a problem; etc.

If a shooter can stop judging himself by traditional standards; likes to train and shoot; enjoys excelling; and is willing to push his personal limits; he will achieve levels of speed and accuracy that were previously unattainable. The catch is that this does require time, dedication, ammunition and quality instruction.

*Moving target shooting with hostages*

*Tire house for advanced CQB training*

*Basic two-man entry drill*

*Good zone coverage and close quarter shooting technique*

## PRINCIPLES OF CLOSE QUARTER SHOOTING

Preparation for room combat and close quarter shooting requires familiarity with basic tactics, physical agility, a controlled aggression and above average shooting skills. Because of the confined spaces in the average room, the shooter can find himself in very close proximity to armed felons, with very little time to evaluate the situation. If the shooter does not react quickly and shoot reflexively, he may well end up a statistic along with the hostages.

The conceptual principles of combat shooting are well known: **Tactics — Accuracy — Power — Speed (T.A.P.S.)**. It does not matter how good a shooter may be, if he makes a tactical error it could prove fatal. Accuracy is relative to the task at hand. One only has to be able to hit the kill zone on man sized targets — not a difficult feat under ideal conditions. The power is inherent in the weapon system, ammunition and the number of shots one fires. Generally two or three to the chest and/or one or two to the head, when the assailant fails to respond to the chest shots. Speed is dictated by proximity, danger and personal ability.

To be able to shoot fast enough, without sacrificing accuracy, requires modification to the fundamentals addressed in Chapter 19.

The key features of the **STANCE** are still **comfort** and **balance** but there must also be the flexibility to move quickly. There is a natural tendency to bend the knees slightly. Do not over exaggerate it by squatting or bending forward at the waist.

The **GRIP** on the weapon, handgun or SMG, should be firm but not overly tight. Excessive pressure on the weapon will adversely affect accuracy. The extent to which the weapon is extended toward the target will be governed by the distance to the target.

**SIGHT ALIGNMENT**, in the conventional sense, will often be impossible because of low light and target fixation. When an armed assailant is pointing a weapon at you or the hostage, it is almost impossible to draw your attention away from the imminent danger and back to the sights. In addition, the distances involved are often close enough to be able to depend on muscle memory and natural WEAPON ALIGNMENT.

Any hope of controlling **BREATHING** on a high stress assault is pointless. At best, the shooter can consciously force himself to relax and breath naturally before entry. Once the shooter is committed to the assault, the pulse rate and breathing will increase dramatically—part of the "fight or flight" response of the human body. When the shooting stops, the shooter can again make a conscious effort to calm his racing heart and ragged breathing.

**TRIGGER CONTROL** will also have to be modified. There is no longer the time to slowly increase pressure for a surprise break. Your weapon must fire at the instant you have a clear shot, and before the gunman can shoot first. With the correct training, the trigger finger will become programmed to respond to visual input and squeeze the trigger without any conscious effort.

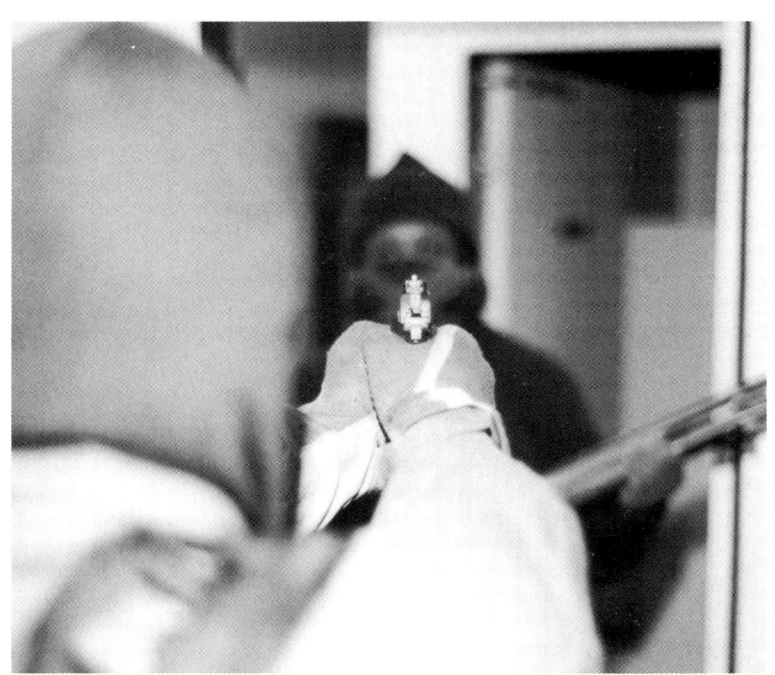
*Conventional aim-fire*

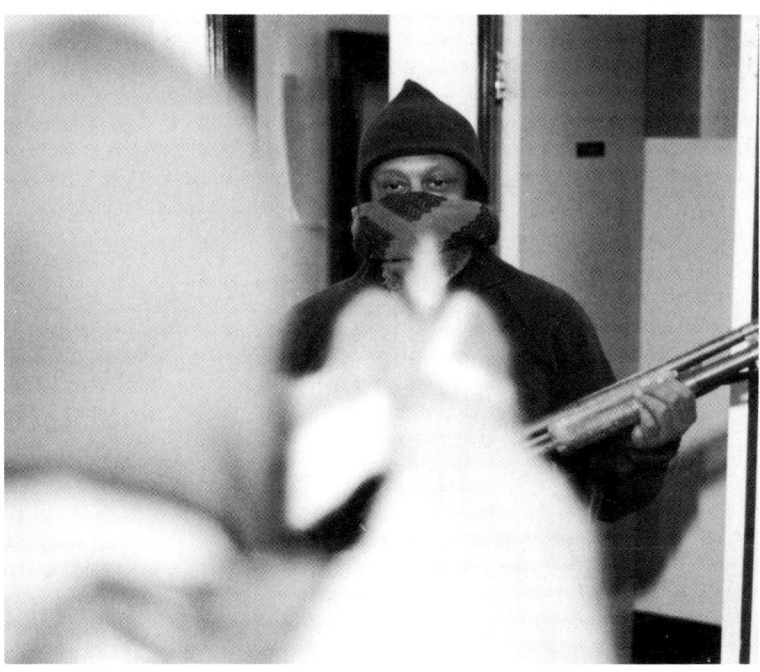
*Natural point shooting — focus on threat*

When engaging **MULTIPLE TARGETS** the shooter will come to depend on this same rapid weapon alignment and subconscious trigger release. Longer shots and smaller targets may require the use of a more conventional sight acquisition and conscious trigger control.

The **SPEED** with which one shoots will be dictated by three factors. The **DISTANCE** to the target; the **SIZE** of the target; and the shooter's personal **ABILITY**. One should never shoot faster than one can guarantee hits, and never try to shoot to others' limits. Misses are an unacceptable part of training and a serious hazard on an operation. Take an additional quarter second to guarantee hits on medium range targets—this gives the gun the opportunity to settle into the kill zone.

**FOLLOW THROUGH** is another fundamental that has little place in close quarter shooting. With time, experience and practice, the shooter will develop the confidence to not even verify his hits on the hostile targets. He will know when the shots feel right and move his attention immediately to other possible threats. Operationally, one should shoot until the threat is neutralized or falls. But with static, non-reactionary targets, one must develop the confidence to shoot and move, especially if speed is of the essence.

## CHANGING FOCUS

There is no one style or type of shooting that will fit all the requirements of a combat shooter. With varying distances and numbers of targets, it is necessary to adapt your shooting style to fit the situation. We have identified five types of combat shooting. The draw, grip and stance remains the same in all situations.

**TYPE 1** is used for a single target at extremely close range. Focus is kept on the target while the shooter depends on natural point shooting ability to guarantee hits. Trigger action is natural and often subconscious.

**TYPE 2** is for multiple targets at close range, as often found in room combat scenarios. The shooter focuses on the targets, confirms index on the first one, shifts concentration to the center-of-mass of each successive target, and again depends on rapid alignment to score hits. The eye may flash back to the slide or sights only when more difficult shots are perceived.

**TYPE 3** is for multiple medium range targets that requires focus shifting from the target to the sights on each shot. The eye must focus on the target for quick acquisition, but then be brought back to the sights for accurate shot placement. The eye may not need to take the time to clearly focus on the sights, but merely register their presence. Finally, do not swing through the targets but index on each one individually.

**TYPE 4** is for multiple smaller targets as may be found in hostage situations and where head shots are called for. The focus again shifts from target to sights. The amount and clarity of the sights will be dictated by the difficulty of the shot. This is the closest type of shooting to conventional aim-fire, requiring clear focus on the front sight with target in the background. Be especially conscious of hostage proximity.

**TYPE 5** is for the most difficult long shot where accuracy is more important than speed. Seldom found in room combat and more common with hostage-taker head shots. Focus is pulled from the target to the front sight for careful alignment. The trigger control will be slow and deliberate throughout the aiming process.

Only through experience and practice will the shooter be able to smoothly transition from one style of shooting to another, reaping the time and accuracy benefits of each. With time, the shooter will also become more relaxed and confident in his ability to guarantee hits under a wide variety of conditions.

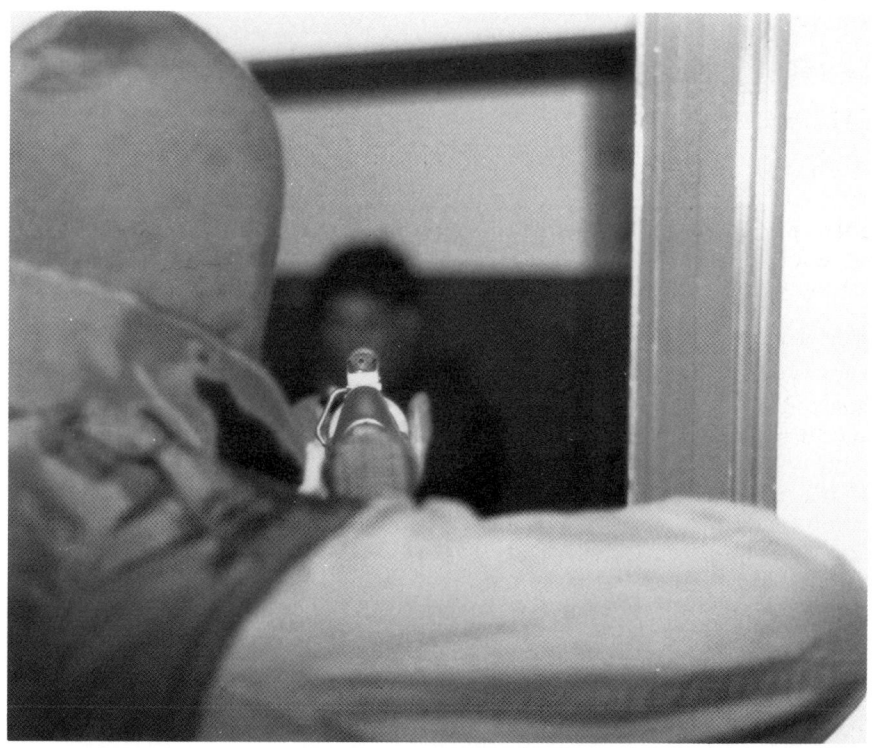

*Aim-fire for the long head-shot*

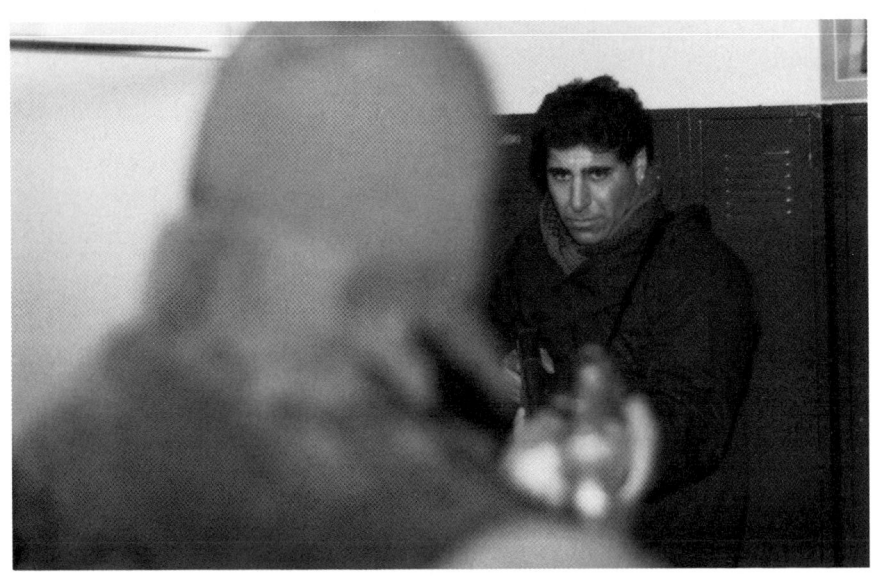

*It is not necessary to see the sights for close-quarter encounters.*

*It is better to focus on the threat.*

## BEYOND ACCEPTED PRINCIPLES

To become a really good shooter, one must step beyond the written word, beyond what is considered acceptable, and even beyond what can be taught. No instructor can stress a shooter or push him as much as he can stress himself. Once the fundamentals have been mastered and the shooter has achieved a well above average standard, then he must look beyond the conscious mechanics of shooting and strive for the level where shooting comes naturally.

There is a level that is reached, when one has shot enough, where the weapon becomes an extension of the body. Muscle memory will bring the weapon to alignment instantly; the eye registers the sights without conscious thought; and the trigger releases when all conditions are correct. It is the same coordination, skill level and reflex action enjoyed by any top sportsman. It is what separates the champions from the masses.

Let us now consider a technique that would be considered heresy by more conservative instructors, who have not been top ranked combat shooters. Traditionally we have been taught to watch our sights if we wanted to shoot accurately. Well, along with many other shooters, we have found that it is not necessary, and considerably faster, if one does not try to consciously focus on the sights. We have found through night shooting and rapid fire exercises, at combat distances, that one could get good solid hits without seeing the sights at all. Even at 25 to 50 yards we were able to focus on the target, let the sights fuzz out, and still achieve center-of-mass hits. Granted, if we wanted to shoot the best possible groups, it was necessary to focus on the front sight. But for combat survival, and maximum speed, that is not necessary.

The advantages of this technique in a hostage rescue role are:

- It is not necessary to take your attention away from a potential threat
- You will be able to better register the assailants reaction to being hit
- You will have better peripheral vision of hostage movement or additional threats
- You will not be handicapped when conditions do not allow you to see your sights
- It is faster at close range

These are also some of the advantages of the laser dot sighting systems. They allow the shooter to keep his attention out on the developing situation and not back on his own weapon.

Now, in actual fact, we may be seeing our sights and registering all the other information because of increased awareness and visual acuity. It is up to the individual shooter to push beyond the accepted teachings of his peers and find what works best for him.

Another area of argument is our firm belief that there is no such thing as Instinct Shooting. Man is not born with the instinctive ability to handle a firearm or shoot. An individual may possess exceptional eyesight, reflexes, coordination and aptitude for firearms handling, but **natural point shooing** is a learned skill. There are individuals that will have you believe they are instinct shooters, but it may just be that they are incorrectly labeling their style of shooting.

Point shooting, without use of the sights, can be mastered through constant repetition of a given movement until muscle memory develops. If a weapon is brought to the aiming position, eye level, enough times, eventually it will return to that position even if focus is maintained on the target. This is not instinct but simply a combination of concentration and muscle memory—a by-product of repetition and positive reinforcement.

Any shooter who has done enough aim-fire and combat shooting has a high probability of hitting a target, even if their sights are not visible. It is called "getting in the groove", and is a valid form of point shooting, without learning a different technique.

*Advanced live-fire hostage rescue drill*

## SPEED

Many instructors and agencies place too much emphasis on speed shooting, requiring their trainees to achieve certain goals within a given time. This can severely hinder the progress of a new shooter. Instead of working on a smooth draw, correct form and guaranteed hits, the shooter is simply trying to get all his shots off in the required time limit.

The speed with which one shoots should be dictated by the size of the target, the distance to the target and most importantly, **personal ability.**

All teams should have standards and qualifications that require shooting under stress and within strict time limits, but these should be realistic standards that are some what immaterial during initial training. The initial emphasis must be placed on **accuracy and guaranteed hits**. Only then can the shooters begin to push themselves and develop speed without sacrificing accuracy.

When practicing live fire entries and team drills, a shooter will always shoot faster than his normal recorded individual shooting times. This is a direct result of stress, adrenalin rush, sensory over-load and peer pressure. With all these stimulants, it is not necessary for the shooter to make himself shoot faster, it will be a natural by-product.

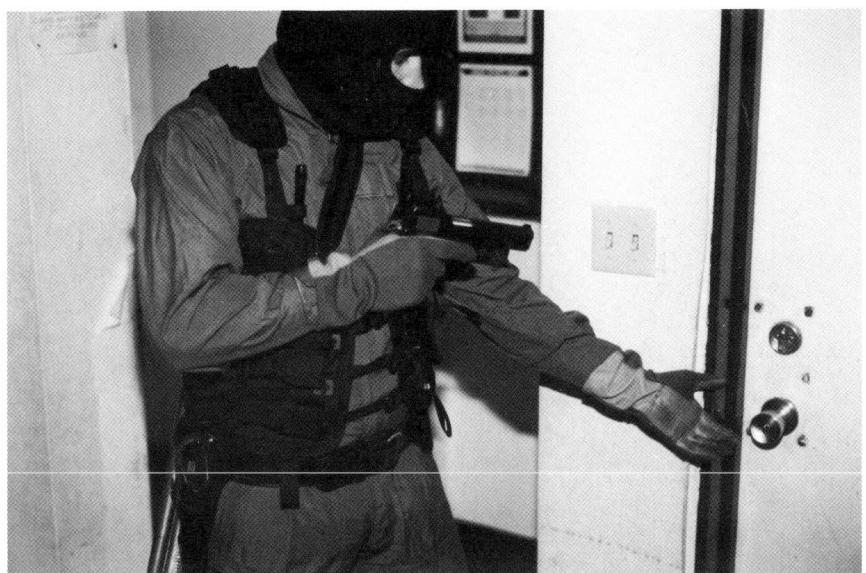

*Note position of the weapon prior to entry*

## MENTAL PREPARATION

Also known as **mind set,** mental preparation is an important part of accurate, controlled shooting. Whether training or operations, a shooter needs a relaxed, positive mental attitude if he is to function efficiently. Excessive anxiety will adversely affect performance.

During initial combat weapons training, the shooter must be carefully coached and encouraged to get the maximum performance possible. Calm instruction, patience and positive reinforcement will boost his confidence and produce better results than negative criticism and an overbearing attitude.

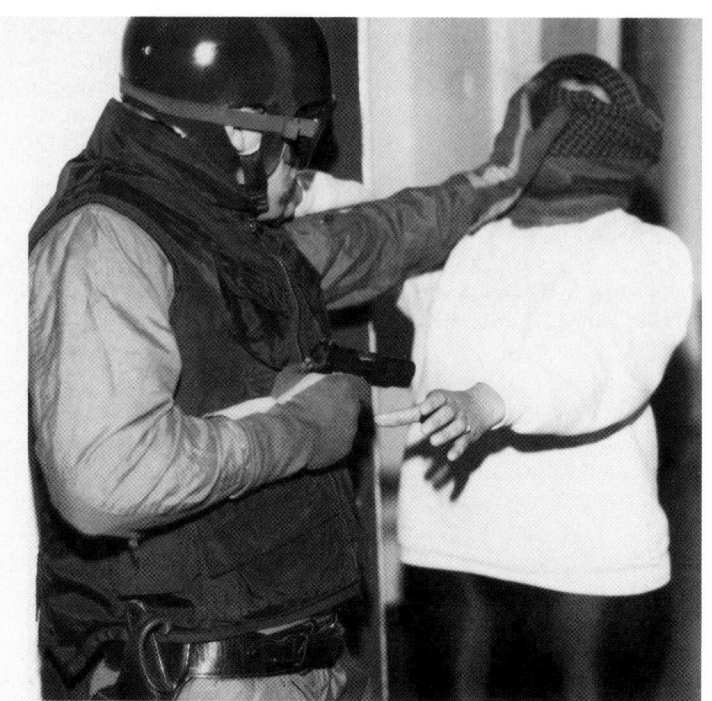
*Extreme close range shooting technique*

A dedicated shooter will eventually begin to push himself to greater levels of speed and accuracy, when he comes to realize that this training is for real. Operationally, his life and that of his team mates may come to depend on his ability. This is a significant stressor, and one that can have very positive side effects.

Even in training, in the face of self induced pressure, peer pressure and the need to meet team standards, a shooter can be subjected to considerable stress. This stress, real or perceived, can have a wide variety of effects on different individuals. For some it will enhance performance, for others performance levels will drop. Each shooter must make a conscious effort to channel this stress into a positive force. Prior to beginning any shooting exercise, the shooter must mentally calm himself and concentrate on the task at hand.

When confronted by the prospect of being deployed operationally, new shooters will often ask, "What is the difference between training and the real thing?" The answer is, "None, but in the real world you don't get any more mistakes."

If the training is based on reality, then the operation should be like one more go around on the range. Granted, the location and targets may be different, but the team drills and shooting are the same. Often times, operations are far less complex than some of the hellish exercises dreamed-up by fiendish instructors.

Then there is the thought and possibility of having to terminate another's life. The military has always understood their task for what it is—KILLING. The law enforcement community on the other hand, has found some less offensive euphemisms for this task.

Police officers are taught to "shoot to stop", or "to incapacitate", or "neutralize the threat", but it comes down to the same thing. Some one is going to end up getting shot, with a high probability of death. Knowing this, what goes through a rookie's mind just before he makes entry? Or more to the point, what **should** be going through his mind?

Before the shooter even approaches the final assault point (FAP), he must have **confidence**. Not the cocky "I am Superman" attitude, but a more mature confidence brought about by a realization that he is a highly trained, well equipped individual, supported by a whole team of equally competent (deadly) individuals.

Now to the probability of killing, and the necessary mind-set. **It is just a job.** He is trained for it, equipped for it, and if the selection process was valid, psychologically capable of it. He is not going in with the sole purpose of killing. He is going in to rescue hostages, arrest suspects and stop anyone who tries to prevent this. When threatened he shoots **TO STOP**—to stop whatever action threatens the lives or safety of the hostages or the team.

The action of shooting (killing), is a conditioned response to external stimuli, and may not require conscious decision making. The shooter should have certain ingrained responses conditioned into his psychomotor memory as a result of realistic training. When confronted with an armed target, he shoots. When confronted by a surrendering target, he covers but does not shoot. This is conditioned response—the programming of the brain to stimulate an immediate response (reflex) to a given set of circumstances.

If a shooter does not have a fast, **reflexive** response to imminent danger, he may be too slow to survive. But with a correctly **conditioned** response, any gunman that dies has brought it upon him-or-herself. They had the option of surrender and cooperation (at least in a police environment), but chose to attack.

Before entering a suspect location, the shooter must accept that gun play is a possibility, and if confronted, he is prepared to respond with deadly force. A shooter who hopes or expects that it won't happen, will be caught flat-footed when it does. He will have to suddenly overcome the shock of reality, recognize the danger, align his weapon and make the conscious decision to shoot. By this time the gunman has already pumped four rounds into him and killed two hostages. This is not the time to be playing the "catch-up" game.

Mental **acceptance** of the possibility, and preprogramming for danger, will greatly reduce the shock and shorten reaction time when the inevitable occurs. Never under estimate your adversary or try to predict how a gunman will react to the threat of death or capture.

There are two old quotations that have some bearing here. "Revenge is a dish best served cold" and "Do not kill in anger." In both cases it refers to the fact that the ability to function efficiently is hindered by excessive emotion or loss of temper. Unlike a football team that psychs-up for a game in the locker room, the shooter must **psych himself down** prior to entry. His actions in the next few minutes, or seconds, must be calm, calculated and precise.

Another mental aspect of special operations and close quarter shooting is **fear**. Fear that we may be killed or injured; fear that we may make an error that costs our partner his life; fear that we may shoot an unarmed man; fear that we may hit a hostage. All are very real fears that have been experienced by all of us at some time. The man that shows no fear is deluding himself. The man that has no fear is probably psychotic, and has no place on a hostage rescue team.

Fear is a healthy reaction to a dangerous situation. It may advise caution or give us the strength and speed to overcome the danger. This is known as "the fight or flight" response. When harnessed correctly and combined with **mature judgment**, fear may well be the deciding factor in a confrontation. The shooter will experience heightened awareness, increased speed, increased strength and an increased ability to absorb pain and injury.

Again, recognize fear for what it is, consciously calm and reassure yourself, mentally rehearse the plan and review options. Then clear your mind and concentrate on the task at hand. Move, stop, evaluate, engage. Ample experience in the shooting house, confronted with realistic shoot/no-shoot scenarios, will better prepare the shooter for the split second decisions he will be required to make.

Reality in training builds confidence. Confidence turns stress and fear into positive forces.

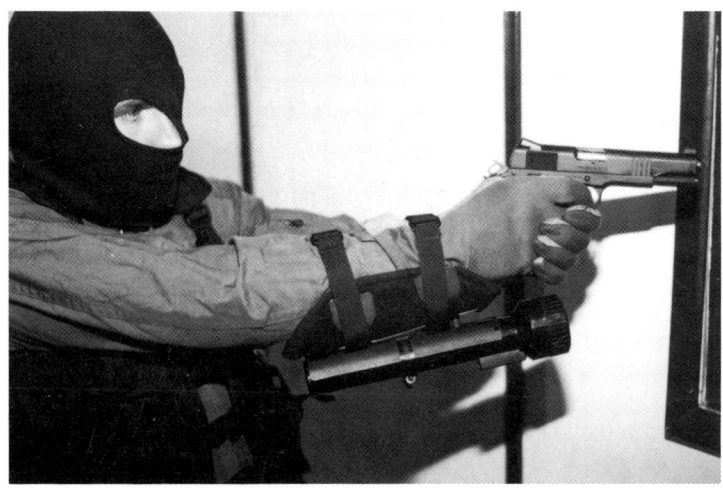

*CQB flashlight arm mount for handgun shooters*

*Pre-entry position*

*Close to medium range shooting*

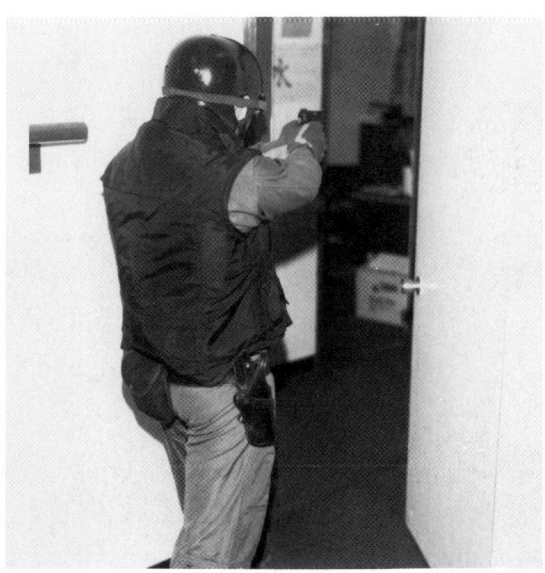
*Aim-fire*

*Snipers are used to secure the assault groups' approach.*

*Sheriff's SWAT team prepare for an aircraft assault.*

# 21.
# ROOM COMBAT

Once the shooter has mastered close quarter shooting, combined with individual live-fire entry, the next phase of training is team drills. Initial team drills are performed in two man units, with eventual graduation to full team, multi room assaults. In studying room combat, we are less interested in the assault considerations addressed in Chapter 15, and more concerned with what happens once entry has been made.

As stated earlier, most tactical operations in urban terrain come down to the individual's ability to go through doors, identify hostile targets and then engage them with speed and accuracy. The principles of the assault are **Speed, Surprise** and **Shock Action**. The principles of shooting are **Tactics, Accuracy, Power** and **Speed**.

## BASIC TACTICS

The first necessity for a successful assault is **KNOWLEDGE**. As Sun Tzu taught in 500 BC, "know your enemy and know yourself." This means that the team will need a thorough briefing on all aspects of the operation, as they relate to the gunmen and the stronghold. For a briefing procedure, see Appendix D in the back of this text.

To achieve the elements of **SPEED** and **SURPRISE**, the team must be able to breach the door and enter quickly and smoothly. The **SHOCK ACTION** will be supplied by the stun munitions, breaching charge or the aggressive domination of the stronghold by the assault group.

The specific actions of the individual assault group members are as follows:

1/ Shooter 1 enters the first room, clearing the doorway quickly. He is immediately followed by shooter 2.
2/ #1 moves directly to the first threatening target and engages him—then continues to clear his side of the first room, or area of operation (AO).
3/ #2 moves to the opposite side of the AO and engages all threatening targets.
4/ When the AO is clear, shooters 1 and 2 will call "Clear, Clear, Go!", signaling shooters 3 and 4 that it is safe to move through that AO to the next room.
5/ The alternative is that shooters 1 and 2 move directly to the second AO when they have cleared the first, being backed-up by #3 and #4.

Keep in mind that one role of the assault group is to draw fire away from the hostages. In so doing, the entry men can expect to take hits, or at least get shot at, as they enter. Hopefully the gunmen's fire will be rushed and inaccurate as a result of the shock action and dynamic entry. Rounds that do find their mark will hopefully be stopped by the team's heavy body armor.

## AREAS OF RESPONSIBILITY

An important aspect of room combat is the use of areas of responsibility, or **individual AOs**. By slicing a room into pie like sections, the room can be cleared far faster than when all shooters try to cover all areas.

Some teams use the technique of predesignating which way each man will move after entering a room. One takes left, the other right, or vice a versa. A faster, safer and more efficient method is to allow the first man to pick his direction based on immediate threat. The partner then takes the opposite side of the room. This can only be done once the assault has been initiated.

The only time a shooter will cross shoot into his partner's sector, is when that shooter has cleared his side of the AO and is needed to support the other shooter. A shooter may also cross shoot when his partner's primary weapon malfunctions in the face of imminent danger.

Though speed is imperative, it is safer if the first pair secure the first AO, and then clear the additional assault elements to move through. By the end of the operation, the entire team is strung out through the building, each covering an individual AO, and all AOs secured. In this way no one is required to move directly through an unsecured AO, risking rear attack.

When negotiating a **linear room combat** problem such as a bus, train or aircraft, the first two shooters will generally enter and prop either side of the aisles. The assault group will then swarm down the aisle, covering left and right alternately, until they reach the end of the aisle, and are dominating the whole length of the cabin.

*Marines are introduced to sniper-initiated assaults during an S.T.T.U. close-quarter shooting program (August, 1990)*

*British SAS assault team enters through embassy window (London, 1980)*

*U.S. Navy SEALS practice live-fire room combat/building searches.*

*Checking doorway prior to entry*

*Corridors can always be dangerous. Note how SEALS split into two pairs.*

## TARGET ENGAGEMENT

Hostile targets are engaged in **order of threat**. This could be influenced by proximity, armament and hostage location.

Obviously, the **closest** assailant is engaged first, and the shooting continues until he is incapacitated. When multiple assailants are confronted, the shooter cannot dwell too long on one gunman. He must hit the first one hard and fast, then move on to his comrades without delay.

Multiple assailants at medium to close range will call for engagement in order of threat, based on armament. A shotgun may be a greater threat than a handgun; just as an assault rifle takes precedent over a knife or club. The exception is where the knife is in very close proximity and the rifle some distance away.

Lastly, criminals or terrorists in close proximity to the hostages will need to be neutralized expeditiously. Before they can recover from the stun grenades and carry out their heinous threats—the execution of hostages. The same stands true for gunmen that pose an immediate threat to other assault team members.

We have found from experience, that the shooters score better hits when they **stop to shoot**. Although some teams, such as the Israelis, shoot on the run and continue to advance on the threat, this only works on very large, close targets. Where multiple targets are concerned, the shooter needs **balance** and a **good stable base** to be able to shoot at top speed. To engage targets in close proximity to hostages, or to guarantee head shots, the shooter will need to stop, aim and shoot. Try both and see which works best for your style and ability.

## SHOT PLACEMENT

**Terminal ballistics** is the study of a bullets performance upon impact with a target. This is of considerable importance when a "quick stop" is called for. Ideally, when lethal force is justified, we would like a shot that drops the gunman instantly. The emphasis is not on killing but **stopping**.

A shot to just about any part of the body can be fatal, especially if the wound goes untreated and the victim is permitted to bleed to death. Unfortunately, the HRT shooter needs a more dramatic and instantaneous end to the problem. A hostage taker, pointing a weapon at a hostage or assault team member, needs to taken out quickly and cleanly. This requires a little more attention to shot placement.

Obviously, a shot(s) to the head is ideal. Especially if the bullet hits the **medulla** or brain stem. The objective being to stop all neuromuscular action from the neck down. When the hit is good, the gunman will drop like a limp noodle.

Unfortunately, not all head shots bring such a dramatic end to a confrontation. The head has some very thick bone covering the brain, and large sinus spaces in the front. There have been numerous cases of head shots that not only failed to kill, they did not even stop the gunman.

However, in training, the shooters should still target the head as their primary **"one-shot-stop"**, so as to develop the necessary accuracy and confidence. If there is any doubt in one's ability to make the head shot, do not hesitate taking the body shot(s). In fact some teams train, like patrol officers, to shoot for **center-of-mass** and only go for the head shot when multiple chest shots prove ineffective.

A third option is to routinely fire two or three times to the chest, and then one or two to the head. If the gunman was wearing a vest, the initial chest shots will have stunned him, giving time for the more accurate head shot(s). It is much faster to target the chest and get the first few shots off, than to take the extra time needed to place the head shot.

Close proximity, hostage situation head shots should also be an integral part of the training program. Shooters should be taught to move laterally to gain a clearer view of the hostage taker. If only a hip or leg is visible, then take the thigh shot and try to pick-up the chest or head shots as he drops sideways.

Walls and doors in the average office or residential dwelling are not good bullet stoppers. If an armed suspect goes for cover, and is partially or wholly concealed, do not hesitate to shoot directly through the barricade. The same applies to car doors, bus or airplane seats, and windows or partitions.

In review. Take the best shot available, head or chest, in the shortest possible time. You can always fire follow-up shots. Shoot until the gunman is neutralized—the threatening actions have been stopped.

## VERBAL COMMUNICATION

In addition to the "Clear, Clear, Go!" used as the assault elements move through the structure, there is a need for other voice commands.

If a shooter experiences a weapons malfunction, he will need to communicate this to his partner with a loud and clear "Stoppage!" This allows the partner to cover the entire AO, as the first shooter clears the stoppage or transitions to his handgun.

When the shooting stops, assault team members continue to dominate the stronghold as team leaders communicate the situation to the command post (CP). For example, "AO 1, Clear," or "Clear and Covering" if there is still occupants in the room. They may also need to communicate "AO 2, two terrorists dead, one terrorist alive," or "AO 3, one team member wounded, one terrorist dead, two hostages alive."

At this point the assault group commander or operations commander can prepare for hostage/terrorist reception, casualty evacuation or crime scene containment.

With secure communications, like those found in the newer model coded and encrypted radios, most teams are able to communicate in Clear (uncoded), without the added hindrance of code phrases and confusing call signs. All personnel must still be cautious about what they say in front of the hostages, prisoners and within ear-shot of the press.

## FAILURE DRILLS

There are several things that can go wrong during an operation, when Murphy raises his ugly head. These problems must be anticipated, identified and incorporated into training scenarios. In the heat of battle, under stress, is not the time to be trying to find a solution to a problem that should have been foreseen.

The first problem occurs when the **primary point of entry** (EP) can not be breached. (Barricaded with furniture or a reinforced door). A second team should already be creating another opening into the stronghold to cover this contingency. Always breach more than one point, even if it is not a multiple entry option.

The next failure can occur when an assault **team member is injured** or incapacitated. The next man in the line-up must immediately take his place, so as to maintain the momentum of the assault. Do not stop and try to render assistance or first aid—that is the role of the medics. Operational momentum requires that the assault continue until the location is secure. In this way the medics can treat or evacuate the downed man in safety. The sooner the AO is secure, the sooner the man will receive expert assistance.

The most common failure is a simple **weapons malfunction**. If the shooter is using a primary weapon such as an SMG, he must immediately drop the useless weapon onto its sling and transition to his handgun. This should be a standard failure drill during all facets of firearms training. If the shooter experiences a malfunction with his handgun, he must immediately clear it and continue (or seek cover). The four most common malfunction drills that should be practiced are:

- Failure to fire
- Stove pipe
- Failure to go into battery
- Feedway stoppage

Another failure that must be trained for is the **failure of an armed suspect to go down** when shot. The most probable cause of this is the possibility that the suspect is wearing a bullet proof vest. But it could also be a result of heavy clothing, excessive fat, drug induced resistance to pain or fierce determination. In all cases, go for the head shot and continue shooting until the suspect drops. Keep in mind that the suspect could be advancing on the shooter constantly, so the shots will be made closer and easier.

The last failure is a **failure of the radios**, either because of abuse, damage or dead batteries. The team must have a contingency for this eventuality, either by the use of voice commands, hand signals or some similar method.

Most potential failures can be identified by studying past operations and by adding realism to training scenarios. "For as we fight—so must we train."

*When one team member has a stoppage, his partner immediately covers his A.O.*

*When one man is shot, the next in line steps forward to engage hostile targets.*

*Snipers should be included in all tactical training sessions.*

*There is no substitute for many hours of live-fire entries.*

*Basic live-fire entry drill. Handguns should be pointed toward the door.*

*Safe weapons handling is a critical part of all close-quarter shooting programs.*

# 22.
# WEAPONS RETENTION

Every patrol officer has experienced the fear, perhaps only in the mind, of being disarmed and having his or her own weapon turned upon them. Walking through a low life crowd; entering a bar or night club; responding to a domestic incident; or wrestling an uncooperative suspect to the ground, are all situations that give the villains an opportunity to get close enough to snatch a gun.

Most police academies and advanced officer survival programs teach a variety of tried and proven methods to prevent a weapon being taken from the holster or hand. These techniques are grouped under the title of weapons retention or defensive tactics (DT).

Unfortunately, few agencies give their SWAT and felony warrant personnel the same degree of attention when it comes to weapons retention as it relates to CQB and room combat. Even the military teams exist under the false perception that if one is armed, then one does not get into fights. The gun solves all problems.

This is not so. In a close quarter confrontation, in a confined space, with several hostile occupants, there is a high probability that someone will make a grab for an assault team member's weapon. The threat could come from either a real suspect or from a hostage or family member.

A criminal or terrorist may go to considerable lengths to escape, especially if facing a long prison term. Your close proximity and the confusion of the situation, may give him just the opening he needs to grab your weapon with fatal results.

Hostages, after a long siege, have been known to form a bond with the hostage-takers (Stockholm Syndrome). This has been brought about by their constant dependence on the hostage-taker for survival and comfort, combined with a sympathetic ear to their views and beliefs. A hostage may see the men in black, the assault group, as more of a threat than the gunmen who have kept him or her alive for several days. If not totally disoriented by the breaching charge and stun munitions, the hostages could pose a threat to the assault group, or at least try to deflect their aim.

When raiding gang houses in search of wanted felons, it is not unusual to find several friends or family members in the same dwelling. These "innocent" by-standers may not be criminally inclined themselves, but they may act to protect a young gang member. Mothers especially, will resort to threats and violence to protect their "little boy" who is really "not so bad", even if he just gunned down a rival gang member, in a public drive-by shooting.

Drug dealers, distributors and manufacturers have also been known to surround themselves with friends and family members. Crack houses are often occupied by users as well as dealers, who may act to prevent the seizure of unbelievable amounts of cash and product. Often times, the presence of infants and small children is for the sole purpose of preventing the raid team from deploying stun grenades. The mothers of these toddlers will have strong maternal instincts when it comes to protecting their off-spring.

Then there is the host of crazies, drunks and idiots who may make a grab for the weapon out of fear, frustration, panic, or whatever rings their illogical bells.

A weapons retention program can be divided into four areas.

1/ The retention of a weapon already in the hand, e.g., handgun, SMG, shotgun or assault rifle
2/ The retention of a holstered handgun when both hands are on the primary weapon
3/ Dealing with a serious felon who is a threat to life
4/ Dealing with a hostage or bystander who gets in the way

With the dangerous felon, maximum force, right up to and including deadly force can be used. With the panicked bystander, one needs to deflect and subdue without excessive force. But make no mistake, this is a life or death struggle. Even the bystander, that is only trying to interfere with your ability to engage a more dangerous target, may contribute to your demise if the real threat is able to bring a gun to bear. Retention techniques must be studied and practiced under ideal conditions, and then applied with force and conviction when needed in the real world.

## SAFETY

Prior to engaging in any firearms retention programs, patrol or HRT, it is imperative that certain safety rules be complied with.
- All weapons must be unloaded and double checked
- Weapons' actions can be taped open or closed with colored tape
- No trainee should have live ammunition on his person, in magazines, pouches or speed loaders
- Training partners should recheck weapons constantly
- Weapons should be rechecked after any breaks or rest periods
- Ideally, inert training weapons should be used

## TRAINING

As with every other aspect of special weapons training, there should be a training progression that guarantees comprehension and ensures safety. There is a potential for injury, even with unloaded weapons—especially, knocks, scrapes, bruises and twisted fingers. Injuries in training mean operators on light duty and being listed as non-operational.

All new techniques should be first demonstrated and then practiced slowly. Only once the trainees have mastered the move should they be permitted to increase speed and intensity.

Combine authoritative voice commands with defensive techniques. Commands such as, "No!", "Get down!", "Do not move!", can be utilized to control the confusion and give people direction.

Study the following photo sequences for an overview of weapons retention. Many of these techniques can also be utilized to clear the aisles in aircraft and buses, where passengers are milling in panic and confusion. The key objective is to never lose control of your weapon, even for a short time.

*Handgun retention*

 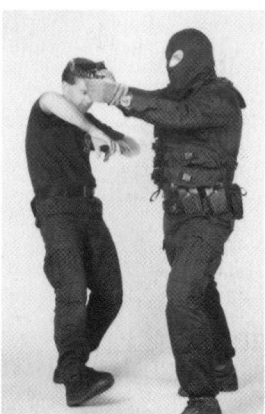

**By-stander interference**

*1.*

*2.*

*3.*

*4.*

*5.*

---

*Hostage avoidance with SMG*

**1.**

**2.**

**3.**

---

**By-stander grabs for gas mask**

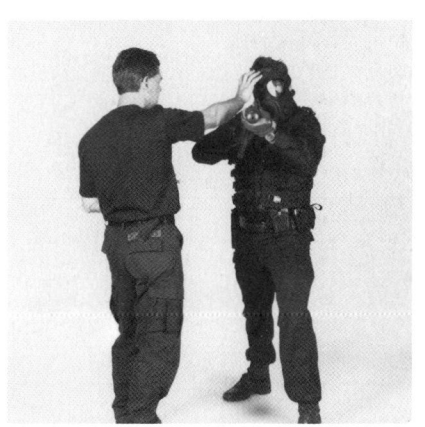

*1.*

*2.*

*3.*

*4.*

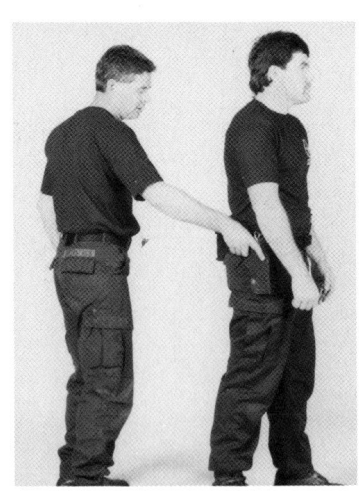

*Handgun retention*

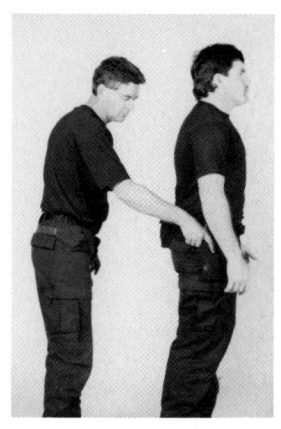
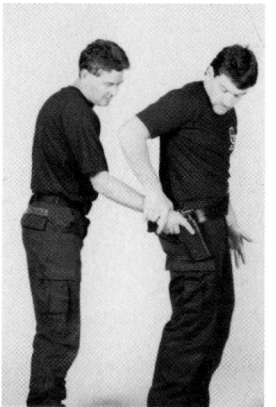

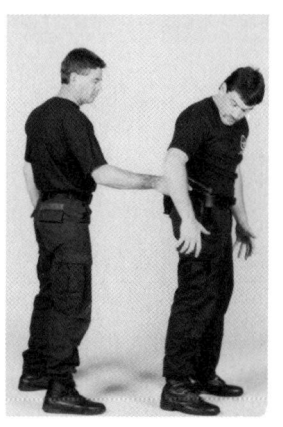
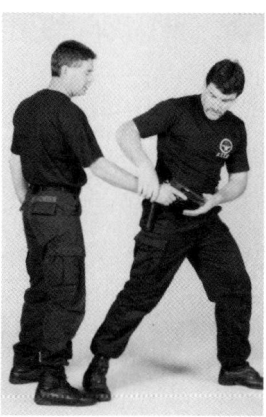

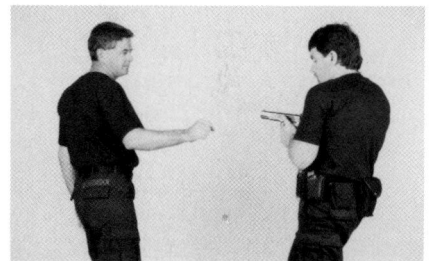

*Handgun retention*

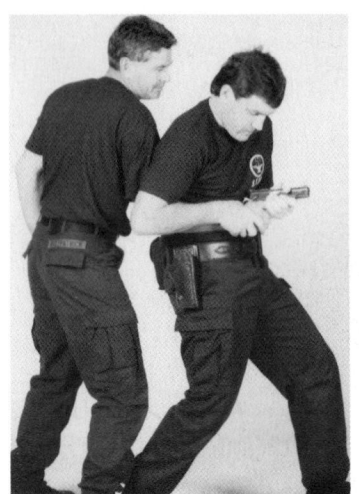
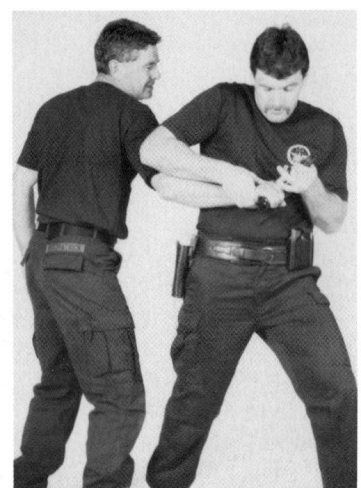
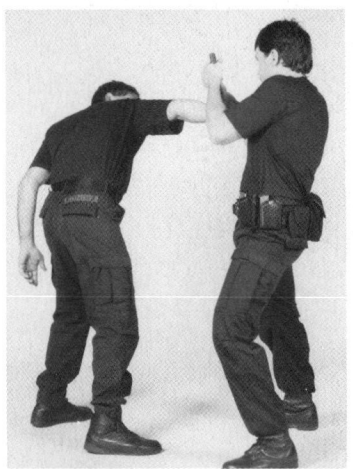
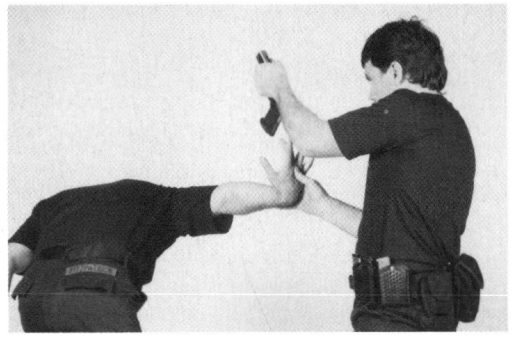

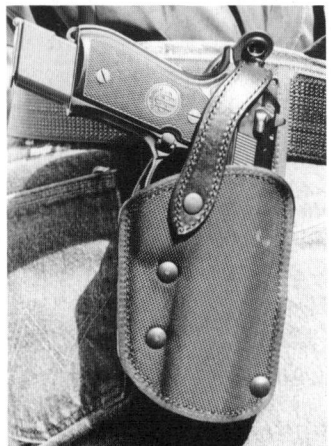

*A good secure holster will prevent most attempts to snatch the handgun (Bianchi)*

# 23.
# POST SHOOTING MANAGEMENT

Once the shooting stops and the smoke begins to clear, the operation is far from over. For some it is only just beginning. It is beyond the scope of CQB to go into all the intricacies of prisoner handling, field interrogation, crime scene containment, preservation of evidence and post shooting investigations, but there are some points that need to be made. The first one being that the assault team has absolute **control** of the situation until the assault group leader passes it back to the operational commander. This transfer of responsibility should not take place until the location is deemed secure and the threat neutralized.

## DOMINATION

The first order of business once the shooting stops is to link and dominate all AOs (rooms within the structure). Experienced teams will do this automatically, while less experienced groups should have a "Dominate!" and "Link!" command built into their SOPs. Assault elements will have already communicated whether their AO is "Clear," or they are "Clear and Covering," meaning there is still movement in their AO.

On the command "Dominate!" all assault personnel will assume a position of advantage in each room, where they can view both hostages and hostage takers, alive or dead. On the command "Link!" one member of each buddy team will move to a door or corridor where he can visually link with the team in the next AO.

At this point, the individual assault elements may be called on for a situation report (Sit-Rep). The report will cover the number and condition of the team members, hostages and terrorists in each AO. For example, "AO 1, two live hostages, one live terrorist, one dead terrorist."

## HOSTAGE CONSIDERATIONS

Obviously, the prime purpose of any hostage rescue operation is to secure the safety of any innocent civilians within the stronghold. This cannot be done until all threats have been neutralized. The individual assault elements must satisfy themselves that all gunmen have been killed, secured or incapacitated, and that none are still in hiding or amongst the hostages. When in doubt, secure everyone with tape or flex-cuffs.

Ideally the hostages should be just as stunned as the gunmen, by the dynamic entry and stun munitions. This will prevent them jumping up, running around and adding confusion to the scene. As added insurance, upon entry the assault team should shouting "Get down! Get down!" to further warn the hostages.

Once the situation has stabilized, the next consideration will be hostage evacuation. Apart from the fact that the hostages may be in need of medical attention and some creature comforts, the building may have been wired with explosives, or be burning from use of pyrotechnic delivery systems. Fire fighters, EOD specialists, doctors and paramedics should be standing by with the reception committee.

When the assault group is ready to evacuate, they will give the signal, "Ready to evacuate." When the command post is satisfied that the hostage and prisoner reception team is ready, they will give the command, "Evacuate now!" At that point, hostages will be evacuated first, followed by prisoners. In the reception area they will be separated and treated accordingly.

The actual evacuation process can go in two ways. One, the assault team forms a chain and throws the hostages from man to man until they are out the door. Two, individual assault team members escort hostages and prisoners out of the structure, plane or train. Prisoners must always be taken out last and separated immediately. Hostages must be matched to photographs and positively identified before being considered legitimate.

## PRISONER HANDLING

This is one area of training where the police teams have it all over their military counter-parts. Law enforcement's day to day encounters with the scum of the earth have taught them that their adversary is a dangerous and cunning individual who must be treated with caution. Caution equates to **Secure** and **Search.**

The type of operation and level of threat may have some bearing on the way the assault was conducted, but prisoner handling is prisoner handling in any field. Whether it be a felony arrest warrant, drug raid or CT operation, survivors must be treated with the utmost caution. On most raids, it would be hoped that the suspects could be hooked up (cuffed) before the stun effects wear off.

There are several threats to the prisoner handlers. They are:

- Gunmen feigning death or injury
- Suspects concealing weapons
- Fanatics wired with explosives
- Hostage takers who have got amongst the hostages

The rule is **SECURE ALL SUSPECTS**, dead, wounded or living. Then **SEARCH**. Always secure before searching, then separate, evacuate and transport. Always have two troopers to each prisoner. One to cover as the other secures and searches. A kneeling position can be used for low threat suspects, but a face-down, spread-eagled prone position should be used for all serious cases. If a suspect wants to fight, and there is insufficient troopers to guarantee physical control, then break contact and prepare to use deadly force.

*British SAS secure terrorist (London 1980)*

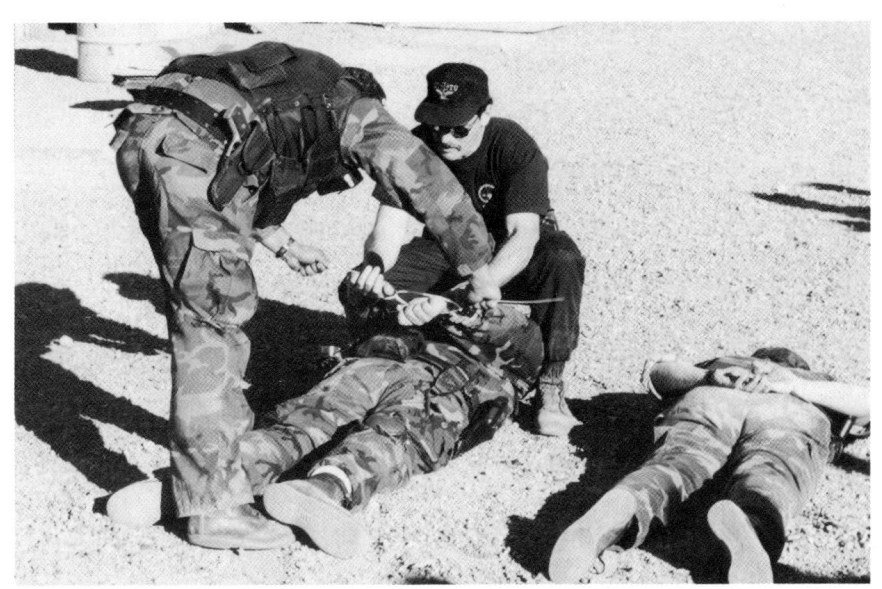
*S.T.T.U. prisoner handling class*

*U.S. Marines practice multiple prisoner handling drills.*

## MEDICAL CONSIDERATIONS

Rappelling, explosive MOE, stun grenades and live fire entry are all high risk options with ample opportunity for accident and injury. Then there is the gunmen to consider. They may have already shot hostages or managed to shoot assault personnel upon entry. Add to this gas, broken glass, smoke inhalation, burns and stray bullets and we have a very high probability that the paramedics or corpsman will be needed.

Injuries can be divided into life threatening, serious and minor, and be treated accordingly. Victims can be prioritized into assault group members, hostages and, a long third, villains. Some teams may put hostage safety ahead of their own, but that is a personal decision.

All injured personnel should be evacuated from the stronghold prior to treatment, because of the risk of fire, booby-traps or hidden gunmen. If this is not possible, an assault team member should fetch the medic and guide him to the victim. Once the casualty is stabilized he should be evacuated promptly.

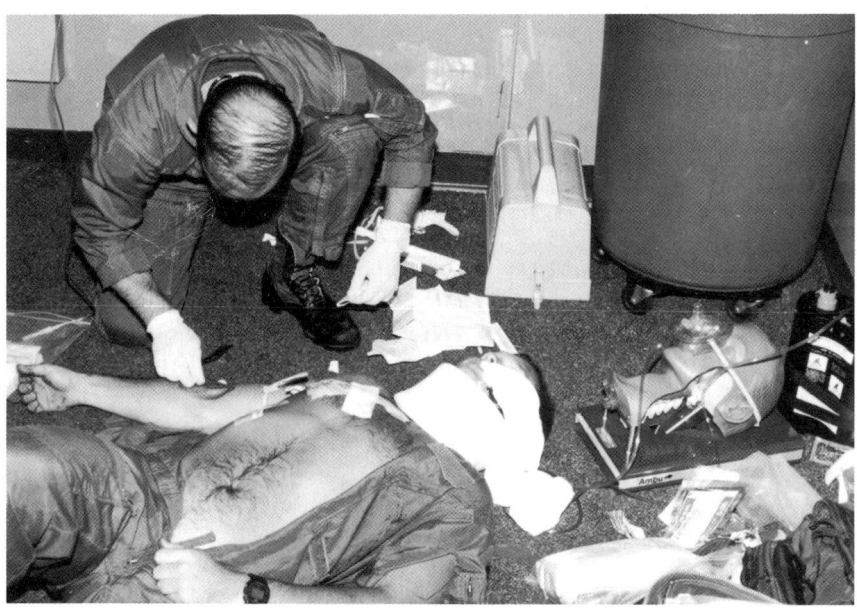

## COMMAND DEBRIEF

Once all hostages, prisoners and casualties have been evacuated, **no one** should be permitted to enter the stronghold until the team leaders or assault group commander have had an opportunity to walk through each AO and get a brief report from each man. This is to ensure all shootings were within policy, and to answer any questions an individual shooter may have.

Statements will be brief, e.g., "I entered through this door, was confronted by this man with a gun (indicating the body), considered my life in danger and engaged him with my weapon."

Alternatives could be, "Upon entry I found three hostages in the corner, no terrorists, no rounds fired." "Upon entry I was confronted by this man, I thought he had a gun and in fear of my life shot him."

Always avoid going into too much detail or stating how many rounds were fired. In the heat of battle, we invariably fire more than remembered. Wait until the weapons are unloaded and count how many rounds are left in the magazines. Secondly, it is advisable not to talk too much in the stronghold, on the off chance that the structure was wired for sound by the intelligence staff and all conversations are being recorded.

All of this is intended to give the assault team a cool down period, to give the assault commander an overview of what happened and to give the shooters a chance to get everything clear in their minds.

## POST SHOOTING INVESTIGATION

Any operation in the continental United States (CONUS), that ends in a shooting, will require a post shooting investigation. Operations outside of the U.S. may be open to international scrutiny and criticism. In either situation, the actions of the assault team, snipers and support personnel must be justified—especially the use of deadly force.

On an international hostage rescue operation in a hostile country, a certain amount of collateral damage may be acceptable—especially if the casualties are local militia or armed civilians.

In the U.S. and on more politically sensitive operations, **unnecessary casualties are unacceptable**. The very term "surgical operation" implies that a cancer is removed with no damage to healthy organs. In plain speak this means, "If they ain't armed, you can't shoot'm." Well, we wish it was that easy.

What constitutes a threat can be far more complex, so a better working definition is the **"In fear of life..."** concept. Any act that poses a threat to the life or well being of a team member, hostage or innocent by-stander may justify the use of deadly force. However, we are not here to contradict any existing policies or procedures. A discussion of agency shooting policy should be an integral part of special operations training. Fire orders should also be given at the final briefing before the assault.

After an operation, where shooting was involved, there will be an investigation that could have far reaching ramifications. Even if it was a totally justified, in-policy shooting, the victim's family will still claim that he was innocent; he was an unfortunate victim of circumstance; he never owned a gun; it was a set-up; police brutality; the police murdered him; he was a good boy; it was racially motivated; ad nauseam...

This should tell the shooter one thing, **KEEP YOUR MOUTH SHUT**. Do not discuss the shooting with anyone except your immediate supervisor and get legal advice if it goes any further. If there is any doubt in your mind, talk to a lawyer. There have been several cases that have ended in criminal proceedings, and a lot more that have resulted in civil litigation.

Fellow team members should also not discuss the shooting until the investigation or inquiry is over. The identity of the shooter should be protected as much as possible, to keep it out of the press and spare his family from harassment.

## THE CRITIQUE

The last and most important aspect of any post operation procedure is the final critique. It is here that the whole operation is debriefed, relived, recreated and analyzed. Photos and videos are studied, stories are compared and different perspectives viewed. Everyone involved gets their opportunity to speak and outsiders are not welcome. The prime purpose is not to lay blame but to identify deficiencies in tactics, methodology, personnel, equipment and leadership.

There are so many variables in a tactical operation that not all contingencies can be planned for. It is simply hoped that the select personnel, fundamental training and available equipment will be adequate to meet the changing needs of the operation.

Many teams critique all training and operational deployments, and then fail to act on them. The true value of the critique comes in the changes that are made. It may be as small as an equipment modification (e.g., adding a light mount), or it may entail the removal of certain weak individuals from the team. So be it. If no serious deficiencies can be identified, then the critique serves to confirm the team's training philosophies and operational methodologies.

In closing, years of benefit can result from a few hours of introspection and constructive criticism. **Do not let big egos get in the way.** The road to excellence is never ending, so the search must be unrelenting.

Whether civilian, law enforcement or military, small arms training must become a regular part of the training routine. Small amounts of frequent practice have proven more beneficial than longer, infrequent sessions.

# 24.
# CONCLUSION

Hand-to-hand combat has been practiced by the warrior class since the dawn of organized conflict. It was used to develop speed, strength, reflex, spirit, and most of all, self discipline. Unarmed combat, to this day, is still a valid training method that instills confidence and discipline in our warrior class—the law enforcement and military personnel who make up our special operations communities. Be they SWAT, HRT or CT these are all small, elite groups of dedicated men who have found courage and purpose in their lives.

In an age of computers, space travel and advanced technology, when it comes to dealing with barricaded criminals and hostage takers, we have not evolved very far. We still find it necessary to utilize small groups of select men who can go in and get the job done. Further more, in the world of special operations, we have found no suitable substitute for progressive combat oriented training to produce good combat oriented troops.

In our present cost cutting, budget conscious times, agencies persist in wasting much needed dollars on high-tech gadgets, when the real need is realistic training, and more of it. A spec-ops team's most valuable asset is the lives and health of its members. This asset can only be protected by prolonged periods of intense training in all facets of close quarter battle, tactical shooting and hostage rescue.

When men volunteer for hazardous duty, they expect that the powers-that-be will make every effort, and spare no expense, to prepare them for the certainty that they will one day be needed. We do it for the astronauts in the space program, but often neglect the police officer or soldier who works daily on the sharp end of reality. When diplomacy fails and the politicians run out of "civilized" options, they are quick to call on the dogs of war. Yet when those same men needed extra funds for training and equipment, those same soft politicians, in their safe offices, were slow to approve the requests or sign the checks.

Police SWAT teams, as with military Special Warfare units, require that their personnel be in a constant state of 24 hour readiness. This is more than just carrying beepers and having equipment pre-loaded into go-boxes. It extends to both the physical and psychological condition of the operators.

History has taught us that nothing better prepares a man for combat than extended periods of realistic training, under the direction of dedicated instructors who have made a life long commitment to excellence. When training time and funds are limited, the quality of instruction and efficient use of range time becomes critical.

If civilized man expects the modern warrior class to fight his battles and protect his insulated existence, then he has a moral duty to cover the costs. The administrator, who approves the checks, also has a responsibility to make sure that the funds are intelligently dispersed. Not on "new toys" that can be displayed to the press, but extra ammunition and training time. The team that substitutes technology for realistic training, hard work and honest sweat is doomed to failure. The team that puts the emphasis on perfecting individual skills, honing team drills and studying their craft, will be the final victors in any battle, whether it be East Los Angeles or down town Tehran.

"... for as we train, so shall we fight."

It is hoped that the material developed by our training group, laid down in this book and the others in the series, will be of some real benefit to anyone actively involved in police or military special operations. We recognize that no book can stand alone as a substitute for competent instruction, hands-on training and field experience. However a carefully researched book can help an intelligent instructor, or team leader, to update existing programs and methodology.

Qualified law enforcement and military groups are invited to contact **STTU** directly, if they would like to take the material in this book, or their CQB training, a step further. We are available for lectures, demonstrations and training programs, any where in the free world. Please make all requests on agency letterhead.

S.T.T.U.
Training & Studies Group
Office of the Director

Mark V. Lonsdale

# APPENDIX A
# ADDITIONAL READING

ADVANCED WEAPONS TRAINING For Hostage Rescue Teams—by Mark V. Lonsdale/STTU

RAIDS, A Tactical Guide to High Risk Warrant Service—by Mark V. Lonsdale/STTU

SNIPER COUNTER SNIPER—by Mark V. Lonsdale/STTU

SRT DIVER a Guide for Special Response Teams—by Mark V. Lonsdale/STTU

The Tactical Edge—by Charles Remsberg, Calibre Press

Practical Shooting, Beyond Fundamentals—by Brian Enos, Zediker Publishing

Practical Pistol—by Dave Lauck, D&L Sports (307)686-4008

No Second Place Winner—by Bill Jordan

Kill or Get Killed—by Col. Rex Applegate

Competition Shooting—by A.A. Yur'yev, NRA

Competitive Pistol Shooting—by Dr Laslo Antal, EP Publishing

Pistol Shooting—by Hans Standl, Kay & Ward Ltd.

Stress and Performance in Diving—by Arthur J. Bachrach and Glen H. Egstrom, Best Publishing

Karate-Do Kyohan—by Gighin Funakoshi, Kodansha International

Dynamic Karate—by Masatoshi Nakayama, Kodansha International

Knife Self-Defense for Combat—by Michael D. Echanis

Fighting Fit (Krav Maga)—by Col. David Ben-Asher, Perigee Books

Black Medicine—by N. Mashiro, Ph.D., Paladin

Sun Tzu/The Art of War—translated by Samuel B. Griffith

*Preparing explosive entry charge*

# APPENDIX B

## GLOSSARY

ACP—automatic colt pistol
AO—area of operation
ATS—anti terrorist squad
AUG—army universal gun
Black Role—military counter terrorism
CAR—colt automatic rifle
CAT—counter assault team
CN—type of chemical agent/gas
CONUS—Continental United States
CQB—close quarter battle
CS—type of chemical agent/gas
CST—counter sniper team
CT—counter terrorist
DEA—Drug Enforcement Administration
DELTA—US Army counter terrorist team
Det Cord—high explosive priming fuse
DVP—distinguished visitor protection
EOD—Explosive Ordnance Disposal
EP—entry point
ESD—Emergency Services Detail
FAP—final assault point
FBG—flash bang grenade
FBI—Federal Bureau of Investigation
FUP—form up point
GIGN—Groupe d'Intervention de la Gendarmerie Nationale
Green Role—conventional special warfare
GSG-9—West German counter terrorist team
Gunman—armed suspect or terrorist
HK—Heckler and Koch
HRT—hostage rescue team
Int—short for intelligence
KEVLAR—a bullet resistant material used in vests
Keep—actual hostage location in the stronghold
LAPD—Los Angeles Police Department
LASD—Los Angeles Sheriff's Department
MM—millimeters
MOE—method of entry
MP—military police
NOMEX—a fire retardant
NONEL—non-electric firing system
Operator—special operations team member
PD—police department
PT—physical training
PR-24—a side handled baton

Re-Org—post assault reorganization
SAS—Special Air Service
SBS—Special Boat Service
SEALs—Sea Air and Land US naval commandos
SEAL TEAM 6—Navy counter terrorist team
SEB—Special Enforcement Bureau, LASD SF—special forces
Shooter—entry man on an assault team
SMG—submachine gun
SOCOM—Special Operations Command
SOG—special operations group
SOP—standard operating procedure
SPEC-OPS—special operations
SRT—special response team
Stick—slang for a baton
Stronghold—structure containing hostage situation
STTU—Specialized Tactical Training Unit
SWAT—special weapons and tactics
TEES—Tactical Explosive Entry School
USMC—United States Marine Corps
USN—United States Navy

*Rip & Ram breaching tool from Newtron Products and U.S. Armor Metro Vest*

# APPENDIX C
# SUPPLIERS

**SWAT EQUIPMENT:**
Eagle Industries, 400 Biltmore Dr., Suite 530, Fenton, MO 63026, (314) 343-7457
Tactical Survival Specialties, 1834 S. Main St., Harrisonburg, VA 22801 (703) 434-8974
The P.R.O. Shop, P.O. Box 201451, Austin, Texas 78720 (512) 339-1393
Shomer-Tec, P.O. Box 2039, Bellingham, WA 98227 (206) 733-6214
K-Zone, P.O. Box 45135, Los Angeles, CA 90045 (310) 337-1037
Richard Cowell Co., Box 538, El Dorado, CA 95623 (916) 622-8333, FAX (916) 626-SWAT

**PROTECTIVE CQB EQUIPMENT:**
Macho Products (RedMan), 2550 Kirby Ave., N.E., Palm Bay, FL 32905-3494 (305) 729-6137
FIST Equipment, 530 W. 23rd St., New York, NY 10011 (800) 332-2535
Glove Specialties West, 6121 Glen Alder, Los Angeles, CA 90068 (213) 469-4494

**TRAINING BAGS & DUMMIES:**
Impulse Sports Training Systems (Impax), 30612 Salem Drive, Bay Village, Ohio 44140 (216) 835-5410

**IMPACT WEAPONS:**
Monadnock Lifetime Products, P.O. Box B, Fitzwilliam, NH 03447 (603) 585-6810

**SNIPER RIFLES:**
Heckler & Koch, 21380 Pacific Blvd., Stirling, VA 22170-8903 (703) 450-1900
ROBAR, 21438 N. 7th Avenue, Suite B, Phoenix, AZ 85027 (602) 581-2648
G. McMillan & Co., 21438 N. 7th Avenue, Suite E, Phoenix, AZ 85027
H-S Precision, 1301 Turbine Dr., Rapid City, SD 57701 (605) 341-3006
Barret Firearms, P.O. Box 1077, Murfreesboro, TN 37133 (615) 896-2938

**SCOPES & MOUNTS:**
Leupold & Stevens, P.O. Box 688, Beaverton, OR 97075 (503) 646-9171
Swarovski America, 1 Kenny Dr., Cranston, RI 02920-8381
Carl Zeiss, Box 2010, 1015 Commerce St., St. Petersburg, VA 23803
California Competition Works, P.O. Box 4821, Culver City, CA 90232 (310) 839-4320

**HANDGUNS & SUBMACHINE GUNS:**
Heckler & Koch, 21480 Pacific Blvd., Stirling, VA 22170-8903 (703) 450-1900
SIGARMS, Corporate Park, Exeter, NH 03833, (603) 772-2303, FAX (603) 772-9082
Smith & Wesson, 2100 Roosevelt Ave., Springfield, MA 01101
Beretta USA, 17601 Indian Head Hwy., Accokeek, Maryland 20607 (301) 283-2191
Springfield Armory, 420 West Main, Geneseo, IL 61254 (309) 944-5138 / 5631
Colt Manufacturing, P.O. Box 1868, Hartford, CT 06101
Glock, P.O. Box 369, Smyrna, GA 30081 (404) 432-1202

**LIGHTS & LASERS:**
B.E.A.M. Co., P.O. Box 634, San Dimas, CA 91773 (213) 592-6156
Laser Products, 18300 Mt. Baldy Circle, Fountain Valley, CA 92708 (714) 545-9444
Tactical Product Specialties, 31855 Date Palm Dr., Suite 3, Cathedral City, CA 92234 (619) 778-7965

**RUST PROOFING:**
ROBAR (Polymax & NP3), 21438 N. 7th Avenue, Suite B, Phoenix, AZ 85027 (602) 581-2648

**CUSTOM HANDGUNS:**
Novak's, P.O. Box 4045, Parkersburg, WV 26104 (304) 485-9295
D&L Sports, P.O. Box 651, Gillette, WY 82716 (307) 686-4008
James Clark, Route 2, Box 22A, Keithville, LA 71047
Bill Wilson, Rt. 3, Box 211-D, Berryville, AR 72616

**TACTICAL RIGS:**
Eagle Industries, 55 Lincoln, St. Louis, MO 63119 (314) 968-4144
Davis Leather, 3930 Valley Blvd., Unit D, Walnut, CA 91789 (714) 595-1526
Safariland, 1941 South Walker, Monrovia, CA 91016 (714) 923-7300
Galco International, 4311 W. Van Buren, Phoenix, AZ 85043 (602) 233-0956
Uncle Mikes, 7305 NE Glisen, Portland, OR 97213 (503) 2545-6890, FAX (503) 255-0746
Bianchi, 100 Calle Cortez, Temecula, CA 92390

**RAPPELLING SUPPLIES:**
CMC, P.O. Box 6602, Santa Barbara, CA 93160 (805) 967-5654, (404) 235-3426

**BREACHING TOOLS:**
B-SAFE Industries, P.O. Box 153-H, Scarsdale, NY 10583
 (914) 723-2553, FAX (914) 725-2925
Newtron Products, 9400 Forest Vista Way, Elk Grove, CA 95758
 (916) 684-1574

**TIMERS & CHRONOGRAPHS:**
Competition Electronics (Pro Timer III), 753 Candy Lane
 Rockford, IL 61111
Oehler Research, P.O. Box 9135-A, Austin, TX 78766

**GAS & STUN MUNITIONS:**
AAI Corp., P.O. Box 3007, Hunt Valley, MD 21030-3007 (301) 683-6420
Def-Tec Corp., 2399 Forman Road, Rock Creek, OH 44084
 (800) 7DEF-TEC

**EXPLOSIVES:**
International Hydro Cut, P.O. Box 86248, North Vancouver, B.C.,
 Canada, V7L 4P6 (604) 980-1415
Omni Distribution Inc., Explosives Products Division,
 P.O. Box 17082, Memphis, TN 38187-0082 (901) 942-3233
Powder Horn Supply, P.O. Box 170, Adams Center, NY 13606

**BODY ARMOR:**
U.S. Armor, 11843 East Smith Ave., Santa Fe Springs, CA 90670
 (213) 945-8941
Point Blank, 185 Dixon Ave., Amityville, NY 11701
 (800) 645-4443  (516) 842-3900
Second Chance, Box 578, Central Lake, MI 49622
 (800) 253-7090  (616) 544-5721
Safariland, 1941 South Walker, Monrovia, CA 91016 (714) 923-7300
Guardian Technologies (800) 462-7880

**TRAINING:**
S.T.T.U.—Specialized Tactical Training Unit, P.O. Box 491261,
 Los Angeles, CA 90049 (310) 829-1738, FAX (310) 829-0868
SCTU, 11A Penrhyn Rd., Mt. Eden, Auck 3, New Zealand (CQB)

**BOOKS & TRAINING MANUALS:**
S.T.T.U., P.O. Box 491261, Los Angeles, CA 90049
 FAX (310) 829-0868

**TARGET SYSTEMS:**
DuelATron (ARS), 12 Skillman Lane, St. Paul, Minnesota 55110
 (612) 483-8113
Caswell, 1221 Marshall St., Minneapolis, MN 55413 (612) 379-2367
Redi-Set Targets, P.O. Box 23084, Jacksonville, FL 32241
Detroit Armor Corp., 2233 N. Palmer Dr., Schaumburg, IL 60173
Speedwell, 40 Rockwood Pl., Englewood, NJ 07631
Por-Ta Targets, P.O. Box 418, Grant, FL 32949 (407) 725-9911
FATS, 110 Technology Parkway, Norcross, GA 30092 (404) 448-7318

**AMMUNITION:**
Simunition, 366 Bruyere St., Ottawa, Canada K1N 5E7 (613) 232-2927
Federal Cartridge Co., 2700 Foshay Tower, Minneapolis, MN 55402
Sierra Bullet Co., 10532 S. Painter Ave., Santa Fe Springs, CA 90670
Hornady, P.O. Box 1848, Grand Island, NE 68801

**ASSOCIATIONS:**
IACP—International Association of Chiefs of Police,
1110 N. Glebe Rd., Suite 200, Arlington, VA 22201
   (703) 243-6500
IABTI—International Association of Bomb Technicians & Investigators,
   P.O. Box 6609, Colorado Springs, CO 80934 (719) 636-2596
ASLET—American Society of Law Enforcement Trainers,
   9611-400th Avenue, P.O. Box 1003, Twin Lakes, WI 53181
NTOA—National Tactical Officers' Assn.,
   P.O. Box 1412, La Mirada, CA 90637-1412
TRA–Tactical Response Assn.,
   P.O. Box 8413, Prairie Village, KS 66208
NASAR—National Association for Search and Rescue
   P.O. Box 3709, Fairfax, VA 22038
ALEA—Airborne Law Enforcement Assn.,
   2313 SW 76th Street, Oklahoma City, OK 73159

# APPENDIX "D"

# MODIFIED BRIEFING PROCEDURE ORDERS FORMAT

1. **STRONGHOLD BRIEF**

    a. stronghold construction

    b. doors - construction
       locks
       opening direction

    c. windows - type of glass
       curtains
       security grills
       height off ground

    d. obstacles - during approach
       outside entry points

2. **SITUATION**

    a. enemy - strength
       weapons
       location
       morale
       intentions

    b. hostages - strength (VIPs)
       location
       age

3. **MISSION**

    a. To rescue the hostages
    b. To secure suspects, drugs, evidence, etc
    c. To neutralize all threats (military)

4. **EXECUTION**

    a. General Outline: A stronghold / bus / train / aircraft assault, conducted in four phases:
       Phase 1: Approach
       Phase 2: Assault
       Phase 3: Re-Org
       Phase 4: Withdrawal

continued over . . .

BRIEFING PROCEDURE (cont.)

Execution:
    b. Detail Tasks: Group 1 -
Phase 1: Approach
    a. Form Up Position (FUP)
    b. Final Assault Position (FAP)
    c. Route to FAP
    d. Order of March
Phase 2: Assault
    a. Area of Operation (AO)
    b. Task
    c. Entry Point (EP)
    d. Alternate EP
    e. Method of Entry (MOE)
    f. Alternate MOE
Phase 3: Re-Org
    a. Link Points (LP)
    b. Hostage Evacuation Point
    c. Order of Evacuation
Phase 4: Withdrawal
    a. Withdrawal Point
    b. Order of Withdrawal
    c. Route to Holding Area (HA)

## 5. COORDINATING INSTRUCTIONS

a. Timings -
   In FUP
   In FAP
b. Actions on Compromise -
   Before given control
   After given control
c. Initiation - Stand By, Stand By, GO
   Alt - FBG
   Distraction
d. In FAP - Codeword
   Cyalume
   Sniper Group
   IR Beam

## 6. ADMINISTRATION & LOGISTICS

a. Weapons
b. Ammo
c. Gas Plan
d. FBGs
e. Medic's Location

## 7. COMMAND & SIGNALS

a. Commander's location
b. Communications channel
c. Seniority

Synchronize Watches
Questions?
Final Fire Orders (Fire Orders Card)

**SNIPERS CONSIDERATIONS:**
One of the sniper pair must attend the orders briefing. If not, the pair must be briefed by the sniper group commander on the following assault related points:

a. Timings
b. Approach Routes
c. FAPs
d. Entry Points
e. When commentary to cease
f. Engaging targets of opportunity
g. Distractions
h. Action on Re-Org / Withdrawal

## SEQUENCE OF RADIO COMMANDS

**INCIDENT COMMANDER**

1. STAND BY, STAND BY, GO

3. RE-ORG (LINK)

5. PREPARE TO EVACUATE

7. EVACUATE NOW

8. ENTERING NOW

9. ALL CALL-SIGNS WITHDRAW

**TEAM LEADER**

2. CLEAR / CLEAR & COVERING

4. HOSTAGE / TERRORIST COUNT

6. READY TO EVACUATE

# APPENDIX E

# ROOM COMBAT GENERAL POINTS

Approach Considerations

Action in FAP

Entry Points

Distraction

Timings

Method of Entry

Alternate Entry Method

Stun Munitions / FBGs

Gas Plan

Keep is known?

Group AOs

Communicating

Dominate Hostages

Hostage Evacuation

Casualty Drills

No Names!

Final Story

Rounds Fired?

Listening Devices

Dress / Uniformity

*Edge-Tek twin radio pack for special operations*

# APPENDIX F

# PREREQUISITES FOR A SUCCESSFUL OPERATION

Political support
Select, motivated personnel
Competent leadership
Discipline
Realistic, mission specific training
Numeric superiority
Superior firepower
Advanced weapons skills
Logistical support
Proven, reliable equipment
Secure perimeter
Control of the news media
Good intelligence
Careful planning
Sound tactics
Tactical flexibility
The will to win
Operational security
Noise and light discipline
Clear communications
Confidence
Patience
Speed and surprise
Shock action
Controlled aggression
Anticipation of the unexpected

# NOTES

# NOTES

# Additional titles available from S.T.T.U.

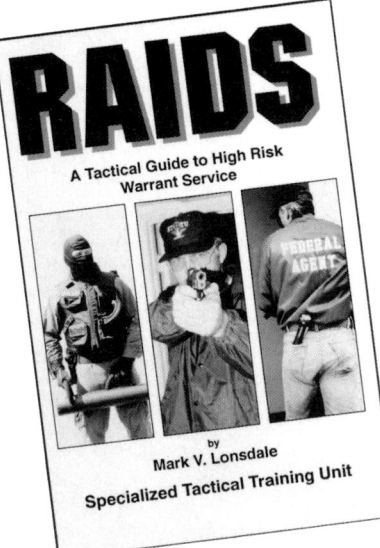